I WANT TO PLAY

I WANT TO PLAY
A HISTORY OF THE SANTA FE
COMMUNITY ORCHESTRA
1982-2007

James Preus

SUNSTONE
PRESS

SANTA FE

Book design by Vicki Ahl

Sunstone books may be purchased for educational, business, or sales promotional use. For information please write: Special Markets Department, Sunstone Press, P.O. Box 2321, Santa Fe, New Mexico 87504-2321.

Library of Congress Cataloging-in-Publication Data

Preus, James, 1931-
  I want to play : a history of the Santa Fe Community Orchestra, 1982-2007 / by James Preus.
    p. cm.
  ISBN 978-0-86534-659-8 (softcovers : alk. paper)
  1. Santa Fe Community Orchestra--History. 2. Music--New Mexico--Santa Fe--History and criticism. I. Title.
  ML28.S33S43 2008
  784.206'078956--dc22
                          2008010391

Published in

WWW.SUNSTONEPRESS.COM
SUNSTONE PRESS / POST OFFICE BOX 2321 / SANTA FE, NM 87504-2321 /USA
(505) 988-4418 / ORDERS ONLY (800) 243-5644 / FAX (505) 988-1025

CONTENTS

PREFACE

hy write about a community orchestra? To professional musicians we're hobbyists. The nonmusical community takes us for granted. Music educators see us as an outlet for their students and an aid to their efforts. I write because I believe we are a unique and fascinating organization. What other organization involves bright talented people who support the organization with their efforts and resources only to produce a product that cannot be seen, which exists for a very brief time, and whose complexities are not understood fully by those who produce it?

No business plan, focus group, or grant request preceded the birth of the orchestra. A couple amateur musicians, who didn't know that starting an orchestra might be difficult, found a willing conductor, recruited a few friends, and made it work. Over the course of 25 years the orchestra has played a hundred concerts and found a place in the musical life of Santa Fe.

All of the hundreds of musicians who have played in the SFCO have their own stories of their lives with music. With a few exceptions, those who play in the orchestra got hooked on an instrument at an early age. Adults, parents, and teachers are always looking for an activity at which children can excel. Those of us who had some talent, who were fortunate enough to find the right music educator, and who got ample social reinforcement for our efforts, found a niche that kept us interested and working diligently to learn our instrument. It worked for me. Through high school, a music education degree, some professional experience, and military duty, music was my life.

For most of us, music was a constant companion as we pursued other careers. There's plenty of evidence in the literature of music education that musicians are well above average in general ability. And so it is for the members of the orchestra. Physicians, physicists, administrators, we have (or had) stressful jobs, and music is an important counterbalance.

Winston Churchill, in a charming little book, *Painting as a Pastime*, describes how his painting took him away from the pressures of his high-profile position; being completely absorbed in his hobby gave him no time to think about the urgent demands of state. Musicians in the orchestra, while they do not guide the ship of state, have demanding jobs. There is an autocorrecting phenomenon about playing an instrument: as soon as thoughts about the job creep into our consciousness while we play, we lose concentration and make a mistake. Psychologists might tell us that punishment is ineffective in guiding learning, but we know better. We cannot think about that experiment, a patient, or an important meeting when we play. Playing an instrument is a wonderful way to relax and regroup.

So the reason for writing this book is to give readers a glimpse of our efforts as amateur musicians. Playing an instrument is a part of my life that I cherish, and I'd like to share my joy with others by writing about our community orchestra.

—James Preus
December 2007

ACKNOWLEDGMENTS

This is a history written by the members of the community orchestra, its music directors and friends, all of whom shared graciously of their time in bringing the past into focus. So, too, have the members of Sunstone Press turned raw material into an attractive publication. My wife, Sherry H. James, a professional editor, improved the manuscript by her careful attention to detail.

INTRODUCTION
I WANT TO PLAY

To play in an orchestra was an exciting prospect in 1982 for a number of enthusiastic amateur Santa Fe musicians. Many were familiar with orchestral literature from their college days or from participating in amateur orchestras elsewhere and they knew how rewarding playing in an orchestra could be. They were too enthusiastic to know it was difficult, so they started an orchestra!

They had just the right mix of ingredients, talent, enthusiasm, leadership, and a musical environment receptive to their efforts. No one that first year thought they were giving birth to an orchestra with a 25-year future, just getting together to play through some interesting music. But the effort took hold, and this retrospective view attempts to chart its beginning and its progress to a healthy and mature community orchestra.

Bob Wingert, the orchestra's first conductor and a wise observer of the Santa Fe scene, believes it worked because Santa Fe is unique. So many fine musicians move here, soloists such as Maya Hoffman and Rosalind Simpson, and musicians with professional and semi-professional experience form a rich pool from which to draw. Greg Heltman, Santa Fe Symphony founder and general director, notes that 20 years ago we didn't expect the high quality we do today; the change is the result of wealthy and sophisticated transplants who expect much from our musical groups. But we also have knowledgeable people who can't afford seats at the opera or concerts by professional ensembles. Those people comprise much of the audience at SFCO concerts.

1

MUSIC IN NORTHERN NEW MEXICO, 1982 A TRADITION

Music was a strong tradition in Santa Fe. In a history of the Los Conquistadores Band, Jean R. Padilla[1] wrote:

It has been called the oldest musical organization in the Southwest, and for seventy-five years it never missed playing for a fiesta parade, but in September 1939 it played for its last fiesta. There was always music in Santa Fe. Many travelers commented on the *bailes* and *fandangos* that were frequent events in the villa at the end of the Santa Fe Trail. Josiah Gregg, one of the early travelers over the trail and author of *Commerce of the Prairies*, observed that "nothing is more general, throughout the country, and with all classes than dancing." Music and dance gave the impression of a perpetual carnival; the musical instruments most frequently used in Santa Fe were the fiddle and guitar, with an occasional small drum like those used by the Indians.

With the establishment of Fort Marcy in 1846, the military band that was a part of most frontier garrisons brought a new sound with afternoon concerts designed to enhance the morale of the troops and improve relations with the community at large. At this the band was a great success. The daily paper frequently commented on its performance and the favorable response of the public to the music "discoursed" by the military brass band.

It was not until shortly after the end of the Civil War that a civilian brass band came to Santa Fe, and it had its origin, at least in part, in the military. Francisco Perez, a native of Chihuahua, Mexico, who had served with the Confederate army as a bugler, participating in Sibley's ill-fated campaign in New Mexico, returned to Santa Fe with half-dozen other young musicians and formed La Banda de Santa Fe. Later the name was changed to Professor Perez's Santa Fe Band, and it performed under several other titles and directors until 1909 when it was incorporated as Los Conquistadores Band. . . .

Through its several iterations, the band survived until 1940, when neither the city nor private donations raised sufficient funds to maintain it; and when many prospective members left for WW II. This was the tradition that Greg Heltman drew upon in forming the Santa Fe Concert Band in1983.

Both professional and amateur musical organizations made up the musical environment in Santa Fe when the community orchestra was formed. They were, and are, integral parts of the cultural environment that brings retirees and artists to Santa Fe. Several professional groups bring audience members from the nation at large (and from foreign countries). Amateur groups provide an attractive outlet for retirees and others to continue their involvement in music. The community orchestra was born into a rich musical environment. That environment had an impact on the community orchestra when it was formed, and on the attitudes of prospective audience members toward orchestral music. Musical organizations in northern New Mexico were launched; some morphed into new forms, some failed, but some survived. The following figure provides an overview of those processes.

Musical Organizations in Northern New Mexico

1846 1940 1955 1962 1974 1980 1983 1993 2007

La Banda de Santa Fe
Los Conquistadores Band
Santa Fe Opera
Santa Fe Concert Band
Santa Fe Chamber Music Festival
Los Alamos Community Orchestra
Rio Grande Symph
(first) SF Symph
Orchestra of Santa Fe
SF Chamber Symph
Santa Fe Symphony
Ensemble of SF
Pro Musica
Taos Community Orchestra
Santa Fe Community Orchestra

Musical Organizations in Northern New Mexico

Professional Music Organizations

The Santa Fe Concert Association

Having begun on April 1, 1937, as a member of Columbia Artists Management's Community Concerts, the pattern of presenting international artists in Santa Fe was established. At that time, Community Concerts provided throughout the country a network of community presentations for which the great artists of the day appeared. The roster of artists from the early years included such luminaries as: Mischa Elman, Gregor Piatigorsky, Zino Francescatti, Astrid Varnay, Rudolph Firkusny, Jennie Tourel, George London, and William Primrose, among many others. The tradition of the great performers and ensembles has continued to this day.

In 1970 the association became independent, wishing to have a greater say in the choice of artists. Since that time it has grown to include youth concerts and special events in addition to its Distinguished Artists Series, has sponsored events of local organizations, and presentations, where possible, of local soloists.

The association has contributed its support to the community through the production of benefit concerts for the Santa Clara Pueblo and the Santa Fe Community Foundation, and through its 26 years of youth concerts for the students of the Santa Fe public and private schools. (Information from the association's website: http://www.musicone.org/index.html)

The musical scene in Santa Fe in 1982 was, in Bob Wingert's words, "uncomfortable." There was turmoil and transition.

Orchestra of Santa Fe and the Santa Fe Symphony

The Orchestra of Santa Fe was a professional orchestra started in 1974. It was actually the second Santa Fe Symphony; the first is described in a later section. William Kirschke was the conductor in 1982. Problems arose about that time, and even today the nature of those problems depends on whose memory and views one accepts. Clearly the "labor dispute" was not just about money.

"Musicians fired in a labor dispute with the Orchestra of Santa Fe have regrouped under a new name—The Santa Fe Chamber Symphony—and plan to conduct a concert series of their own." John Landis conducted the first concert. Thirty-four of 39 musicians were former Orchestra of Santa Fe musicians. Greg Heltman is orchestra manager." (*Santa Fe New Mexican*, Sept. 3, 1984)

In 1985, in an article titled "The Orchestra Wars," Craig Smith wrote: "Last September, Kirschke told the [Santa Fe] *Reporter* that the founding of the Chamber Symphony was 'a constructive act,' and Heltman recently commented that, as far as the Chamber Symphony was concerned, 'We don't see any reason why we both can't exist.' In a letter dated Nov. '86 to Artemus Edwards, a bassoonist with the Chamber Symphony, Sylvia Ball, then the president of the Orchestra of Santa Fe's board of directors, informed him, "We have no desire to thwart your attempts to enrich Santa Fe with your series of concerts, and hope you will give us the same consideration." ... Kirschke's remarks about the Chamber Symphony were considerably less polite than Ball's. "They [the Chamber Symphony] have no credibility, no viability" he said. "No one came to their youth concert, and no one came to the concert last week. . . ." (*Santa Fe New Mexican*, February 20, 1985)

The uneasy truce lasted for ten years. William Kirschke resigned from the Orchestra of Santa Fe in 1993, and the Ensemble of Santa Fe and the Santa Fe Chamber Symphony merged and became the Santa Fe Symphony.

Why was the contention between professional orchestras a factor in the birth of the community orchestra? One can speculate that there was tension in the musical community and to some extent in the audience for orchestral music. Along came this easy-going amateur orchestra that had no ambition to compete with professional groups and which welcomed any and all to its informal concerts.

The Orchestra of Santa Fe and the Santa Fe Symphony were the two ongoing and regularly scheduled concert series through the year in Santa Fe. Other less regular and summer-season professional musical organizations enriched the overall environment of the musical culture in Santa Fe, but were probably not contributors to the tension in professional groups previously noted.

The community orchestra was born in a rich musical environment; that environment conditioned members of the community to value classical music and provided an incentive for those seeking a retirement community to choose Santa Fe. Such immigrants included some with talent and experience as orchestral musicians. Other contributors to the professional musical environment were the Santa Fe Opera, and the Santa Fe Chamber Music Festival:

Santa Fe Opera

The Santa Fe Opera is a national treasure, thanks to the leadership of the late John Crosby, its founder and director until 2004, and his successor, Richard Gaddes.

Each July and August since 1956, opera lovers have been drawn to the northern New Mexico mountains to enjoy productions by one of America's great summer opera festivals. More than 130 operas have been performed here, including American premieres of more than 40 works, including *Lulu, The Cunning Little Vixen, Capriccio,* and *Daphne.* Casts are drawn from the world's most talented young singers; conductors, directors, and designers are international as well. A small opera-titles screen in front of every seat follows the stage action in either English or Spanish. The 2007 season included *La bohème, Così fan tutte, Daphne,* the American premiere of Tan Dun's *Tea: A Mirror of Soul,* and *Platée.*

Santa Fe Chamber Music Festival

Since it started in 1972, the Santa Fe Chamber Music Festival has become one of the world's pre-eminent music festivals dedicated to artistic excellence and innovation and set amid the splendors of the Sangre de Cristo Mountains. With legendary cellist Pablo Casals as honorary president, the 1973 inaugural season hosted 14 artists performing six Sunday concerts in Santa Fe and additional appearances in other New Mexico and Arizona communities. In 2007, the festival celebrated its 35th anniversary by continuing a tradition of presenting distinguished musicians, along with emerging young talent, during its six-week season, for more than 80 concerts, recitals, master classes, youth concerts, and open rehearsals.

Sheldon Rich, the Chicago native who founded the festival along with his wife, pianist Alicia Schachter (they also served as festival director and artistic director, respectively), believed he had the answer:

"I think this has a lot to do with the change in format

of chamber music today in America," he says. "It's more exciting programming, more varied instrumentation, younger artists and resident composers taking part, also the upsurge of interest in contemporary music. It's a whole new era."

Other Amateur Music Organizations

In Santa Fe, in 1982, there were no organized groups that provided opportunities for amateur musicians to participate in making music. The Santa Fe Concert Band was in the process of being resurrected, but that provided an outlet only for woodwind and brass players, and relatively few at that. However, that had not always been the case, for there had been a lively amateur music scene in the 1960s.

The Rio Grande Symphony and the (first) Santa Fe Symphony

The line between amateur and professional organizations isn't always clear. In this instance a community orchestra morphed into a semi-professional group.

In the late 1950s Doctor H. R. Landmann, a prominent Santa Fe physician, and a few others, wanted to found an orchestra. They knew of John Hiersoux and asked him whether he would do so. Hiersoux and his wife had a career as duo pianists and had been active in the Charleston music scene. The Rio Grande Symphony was active for seven years. The first Santa Fe Symphony was organized in 1962, including a number of players from the Rio Grande Symphony. Marylinda Gutierrez, active today in the Santa Fe Community Orchestra, was its flutist. In 1962 Bernard Rubenstein, who had recently completed graduate studies at Yale and was studying conducting in California, through a violinist friend was invited to conduct a concert of the symphony. It was a success, and he was hired, at the grand sum of $2,000 for the season, to be the music director beginning in 1963.

The 1960s were an exciting time for music in Santa Fe. In his two years with the Santa Fe Symphony, Bernie Rubenstein described a new English translation for the Beethoven *Fantasie for Piano, Chorus and Orchestra* by Winfred Scott, famous poet (and Joel Scott's father), and the premiere of *Fantasy Aborigine, No 1*, Louis Ballard's first orchestra piece, presaging his status as noted composer. Ballard was the timpanist in the symphony. Members of the board of the symphony looked like a Who's Who of distinguished members of the community.

Strange are the ways musicians move about: John Hiersoux was a friend of Erich Leinsdorf; Leinsdorf vacationed in Santa Fe; Hiersoux introduced Rubenstein to Leinsdorf, who, when Rubenstein told him he wanted to be a conductor, advised him to leave Santa Fe for areas with greater visibility to the musical world. In spite of the fact that his salary was raised to $3,000, Rubenstein left after the 1963-64 season, to conduct the Rhode Island Philharmonic. The Santa Fe Symphony lasted a couple more years.

Los Alamos

Our neighbor on the hill, Los Alamos, had a different history. During the World War II Manhattan project to develop the atomic bomb, distinguished scientists were brought to the closed Los Alamos community. Many were accomplished musicians as well as distinguished scientists. Robert Brode, in the movie *The Day After Trinity* (1981), notes:

> We had a good deal of music at Los Alamos, organized and unorganized. Walking along the roads in the evening, we heard the strains of Bach or Mozart

that filled the air. High up in the mountains, radio reception was poor, but we had our own radio station in the last year. The station used records from the collections of residents, and our otherwise quiet mesa was soon saturated with the world's best music.

A lot of physicists and their wives were classically trained musicians, so there were many recitals and an annual chorus singing of Handel's *Messiah*. Edward Teller was particularly brutal on everyone's sleep cycle, with his odd hours, workman-like style, and broad repertoire.

The Manhattan project left its mark on classical music in Los Alamos. A number of the scientists who participated in the classical music scene remained in Los Alamos, either with the Los Alamos National Laboratory or as retirees, and supported attempts to keep classical music alive.

Rosemary O'Connor, a founding member of the Los Alamos Symphony Orchestra, provided the following history of the Los Alamos Symphony Orchestra in a 2007 personal communication:

The origins of the symphony date back to the Manhattan Project in the 1940s. The first organization began as a small chamber music ensemble that grew to about 30 musicians. The players were both military and civilians, and about half were wind players. Fortunately, the first director was a man named Robert Dike, a horn player, who was able to arrange the music to fit the players who were available.

Conductors with long tenures were Don Beene, Ernest Kalmus, Robert Wingert and, currently, Michael Gyurik. Others who conducted one or more concerts were Kathleen Manley, John O. Winks, Harold Weaver, Frank Pinkerton, Patricia Gambell, Alan Malmberg, Hans Schmettau, Hans Lange, John Hiersoux, Kurt Frederick, John Seagrave, C. Rex Eggleston, Sidney Brantley, Thomas O'Connor, William C. Houston III, Jan McDonald, Don Gerheart, and John Ward.

The ensemble was successful and grew in size, and began calling itself the Community Orchestra in 1947. Financial support for music and other expenses came from the "Special Services" of the United States Army.

In 1948 the Atomic Energy Commission took over from the Army, and helped the orchestra for a number of years. During this year, the orchestra also changed its name to the "Los Alamos Sinfonietta." They continued to be successful, and the sinfonietta presented at least two concerts every year for the next four decades.

The organization changed its name again in 1990 to the "Los Alamos Symphony Orchestra," and formally became a nonprofit corporation. Since then, the symphony has presented three concerts each year, and its members have participated in orchestral support for the Los Alamos Choral Society and the Los Alamos Light Opera.

The Los Alamos Symphony Orchestra has been an important part of the cultural life of Los Alamos for nearly 60 years. It has provided the opportunity for members of the community and advanced students to play the masterworks of classical music. And these musicians have shared their music with the community, and will be doing so for the next 60 years!

The Los Alamos Community Winds was also active; Jan McDonald, then the band teacher at Los Alamos High School, was its director from 1970-90; Ted Vives is now the director.

Chorus of Santa Fe

The Chorus of Santa Fe, conducted by Landon Young, was formed in 1978. It performed three or four concerts a year, usually in St. Francis Auditorium, sometimes accompanied by an orchestra. The chorus morphed into the Santa Fe Symphony Chorus in 1984. Michael Golden and Pat Greathouse, current members of the SFCO, were members of the chorus.

Taos

Taos also had a history of excellent classical music. Harold Geller, a violinist in the Santa Fe Community Orchestra since its third concert, started the New Mexico Music Festival in Taos in the 1970s. For the first five years it was a chamber orchestra in Taos. Politics made it difficult to continue in Taos. Music at Angel Fire was the offshoot, beginning in 1978. Faculty came from colleges all over the country. Today Music at Angel Fire is a nationally known venue for distinguished professional musicians.

The Taos Community Orchestra, in association with the Taos Choral Society, had a good run from the 1980s until early 2000s, attracting musicians from Santa Fe and Albuquerque as well as its core in Taos. It performed regularly at Adams State College in Alamosa and several small towns in northern New Mexico as well as in Taos. Unfortunately, it has been inactive the past several years.

Amateur Music in Santa Fe

As noted previously, the Santa Fe Concert Band was just starting its comeback in 1983 and was not a factor in the birth of the community orchestra. There were no other organizations that provided an outlet for amateur musicians. There were informal opportunities, however.

The Aeolian Woodwind Quintet

Mary Ann Martinez, Flute; Daniel Koenig, Oboe; Marcia Meyers, Horn; Michael Golden, Clarinet; Margo Spencer, Bassoon.

The Aeolian Woodwind Quintet was formed of the principal woodwind players during first year of the community orchestra; three of the members still play in the orchestra 25 years later.

The quintet performed Agay's *Five Easy Dances,* on the June 12, 1983, concert of the SFCO. It also performed at benefit programs during the first year, representing the orchestra, including at Museum Day on the Plaza in May 1983.

Informal Chamber Music Groups

String ensembles that included semi-professional and professional players who did not play in the community orchestra met routinely but did not offer an opportunity for most string players in the orchestra. Friday mornings were regular meetings at Mildred Hemsing's home that included Mildred, Jack Miller, John DiJanni, Meg Neher, Pat Greathouse, and others.

Recorder Groups

The Santa Fe Recorder Society was an active group in 1982. Lisa Van Sickle, Mary Ann Martinez, and others played in the Santa Fe Recorder Society for several years before the orchestra started.

Significance of the Musical Environment

In 1980 Santa Fe County had a population of 75,360. Even today (2007), the City of Santa Fe population was estimated to be 66,476. Many, but not all community orchestras, those in the same category used by the American Symphony Orchestra

League, based on annual budgets, are in large communities. Three other orchestras similar to the Santa Fe Community Orchestra are celebrating their 25th anniversaries in 2007. The Brazosport, Texas, orchestra plays six concerts a year in a community of (year 2000) 52,258. The Glacier orchestra in Kalispell, Montana, plays six concerts and pops concerts in a community of (year 2000) 14,263. By contrast, the volunteer Reno, Nevada, pops orchestra plays four formal concerts in a community of 180,480. Community size does not seem to correlate with program. What does?

Three factors suggest themselves as supportive of the birth and growth of the community orchestra in Santa Fe in 1982:

Musical Environment

For a small community, relatively isolated from major population centers, the number and quality of musical groups, as outlined previously, are unique. Three are of national importance: the Santa Fe Opera, the Santa Fe Chamber Music Festival, and (in Taos) Music from Angel Fire. It is a rich musical environment in the summer.

Sophisticated Population

It is commonly acknowledged that New Mexico is a poor state, with low income levels and large numbers of children below the poverty level. Santa Fe is different. Figures for 1980 are not easily available; the 2005 estimated median household income in Santa

Fe was $45,177, not significantly different from the national median. However, the median home price was $282,700, or 137% higher than the national average. Los Alamos is even more dramatic; median 2005 income was $71,536, or 70% above the national average. It is not a large leap to assume that education is related to affluence, or that education is related positively to appreciation for the arts.

Support

The Santa Fe Symphony, like most professional music organizations, gets about 40% of its income from ticket sales. It is in the black and building its endowment. The other professional groups are in a similar situation. The community has supported the Desert Chorale, started in 1982, as well. With a few exceptions, the community orchestra shares the fall to spring calendar with the Santa Fe Symphony, but they are in different financial tiers and draw support from different segments of the Santa Fe population. Voluntary contributions by those attending 2006-2007 SFCO performances were $3,420, or 6.25% of total income, considerably less than 40% of total income.

Santa Fe is a place where classical music thrives. The community orchestra is fortunate to exist here in the reflected admiration that draws appreciative audiences to its concerts.

2

GETTING STARTED

Anne-Lise Cohen, who with Jody Ellis was the driving force in establishing the community orchestra, wrote:[2]

In the spring of 1982, Robert Wingert agreed to conduct an amateur orchestra if someone would be willing to bring such a group together. On April 16, a notice was sent out by Anne-Lise Cohen and Jody Ellis inviting interested amateur musicians to come to a meeting on April 30 to discuss forming an amateur orchestra. The response revealed a sizable group of people eager to play symphonic music. Although the group made up a somewhat lopsided instrumentation (lots of flutes and clarinets, but short on strings and percussionists) it was sufficient to start and a first rehearsal date was set for May 12. The Santa Fe Community Orchestra was born and immediately faced with the first major problem of finding a suitable rehearsal space. Ms. Jean Salas, head principal of Capshaw Junior High School, with the gracious cooperation of Mr. David Trujillo, Capshaw's music teacher, offered the school's band room for weekly rehearsals. The orchestra now had a home and a conductor, but no funds whatsoever. The members started to raise money from friends and businesses and with a $500 donation from Gertrude Mary Joan Haig the foundation for the operation of the orchestra was laid.

SANTA FE COMMUNITY ORCHESTRA

Organizational Meeting
April 30, 7:30 p.m.
First Presbyterian Church
Santa Fe

Agenda

I   Welcome and Introduction

II Nature and Goals of Organization

      a.   non-profit amateur orchestra (except conductor)
      b.   high quality performance
      c.   community service
      d.   first rehearsal, May 13, 7:30 p.m., Capshaw Jr. High School, 351 East Zia Road, Santa Fe. Bring your own stand and plenty of enthusiasm, and we'll have a ball.
      e.   First performance

III Presentation of Pro-tem Board

IV Finances

V   Robert Wingert on Rehearsal Procedure

VI Questions and Answers

VII Coffee and Cookies and Meeting Each Other

Organizational Meeting

Soon word got around and musicians from Los Alamos, Las Vegas, Española, and Taos began to make the long trip to rehearsals and concerts. They are still with the orchestra. Several professional musicians and music teachers joined the orchestra and have continued to play with it. Along with them came a number of high school students who benefit from the experience of playing symphonic music. (Note: In recent years high school students have an excellent opportunity to play with the Santa Fe Youth Symphony, founded in 1994, and so no longer play with the community orchestra.)

With the encouragement and cooperation of Dr. Tom Chavez, in charge of the Palace of the Governors, the first public concert was held on July 5 on a warm moonlit evening in the patio of the Palace of the Governors. It was billed as a "Pillow Concert" and adults and youngsters made themselves comfortable on blankets and pillows on the grass while enjoying the music. This was not only the debut of the new orchestra, but was also the first time a symphony orchestra had performed at the Palace of the Governors in the 372 years of its history.

The first concert was quite a success. Willard Chilcott, a "can-do" cellist, and Anne-Lise's son rigged a tarp over a "stage" (the orchestra sat on the ground). To make some money, one of the originators of the Buckaroo Ball arranged for food—Lady Rodeos provided a barbeque. Audience members took their purchases to their blankets or pillows. People, including whole families, came with chairs. Why so popular? There weren't so many things to do in 1982 as there are today, and so those first concerts were packed. Anne-Lise: "Other musical performances were expensive, but this was free. It was like a picnic. Tom Chavez's enthusiasm was wonderful." Mary Ann Martinez remembers that a bird sang right along with the orchestra. The setting was difficult for musicians; they dashed into the portal when it rained (as did audience members). Hence, the concert lasted a long time.

The premiere concert was such a success that the orchestra was asked to repeat the concert on September 19, 1982.

For Love, not Money

By ROBERT GRAYBILL

"It's a kind of 'love' orchestra," Jodie Ellis said. "We're simply doing it for pleasure," she added, referring to the city's newest cultural institution, the **Santa Fe Community Orchestra,** which will hold its premiere concert on Monday, July 5, in the courtyard at the **Palace of the Governors.**

Comprised of approximately 40 amateur musicians, the community orchestra is the brainchild of Anna Lisa Cohen, who first thought of putting such a group together last summer.

"Anna Lisa first had the idea for an orchestra where beginners, that is *skilled* beginners, and amateurs could play," said Ellis. "That was last summer. But nothing was done about it till February."

Then Cohen interrupted. "One of the reasons it didn't go on was because we could find no one to conduct." In February, Cohen found the answer to her prayer in Robert Wingert, who will conduct his tyro band next Monday in Beethoven's "Turkish March from the Ruins of Athens"; Haydn's Symphony No. 104, "London"; Brahms' Hungarian Dance No. 5; Johann Strauss' "Emperor Waltz"; and selections from Liadov's "Eight Russian Folk Songs."

The choice of pieces for the concert was dictated by two factors. As Cohen explained, "We wanted something that was light-classical, something easily accessible," and, as Wingert amended, "They were all in the New Mexico State Library."

Wingert, who is also the musical director of the fledgling orchestra, is a local clarinetist and clarinet teacher who has played with the Atlanta Symphony, the Southwest German Radio Orchestra and the orchestra of the Santa Fe Opera.

A graduate of the Cleveland Institute of Music and the Indiana University School of Music, Wingert has spent most of his career as a professional musician; he took up the baton only last winter to conduct the Los Alamos Sinfonietta, that town's amateur orchestra.

According to Wingert, most of the orchestra members come from Santa Fe, while a few are members of the Los Ala-

Robert Wingert

mos Sinfonietta. Wingert also categorized most of his players as people who once studied an instrument but had to lay it aside to pursue a career. "It's wonderful to see the excitement of the people who get to play," Cohen remarked.

It is the hope of Cohen, Ellis and Wingert that the Santa Fe Community Orhcestra will continue to play throughout the year. Already the trio is planning two concerts for the coming season.

The orchestra's outdoor concert — "Pray for no rain!" Cohen exclaimed — will take place at 8 p.m. Tickets are priced at $3 for the general public and $1.50 for students and senior citizens. "We don't want to charge $10 a ticket," Ellis explained. "We want to bring music to the clientele who can't afford that price."

When asked why Santa Fe needs another orchestra, Ellis shot back, "For the people!"

The Santa Fe Community Orchestra will perform at 8 p.m. in the courtyard of the Palace of the Governors (bring blankets and pillows) on Monday, July 5. There will be an open dress rehearsal on Thursday, July 1, in the courtyard at 7:30 p.m.

Tickets for the concert, which are $3 and $1.50, can be purchased at the door (the blue doors on Lincoln Avenue). Anyone wishing to help the orchestra may call 982-4022 or 983-6865. The orchestra is still actively recruiting string players.

For Love, Not Money

Early Years

Performances

As part of the Scandinavian Today festival in Santa Fe, conductor Wingert scheduled the Sibelius Second Symphony for the orchestra's first formal concert in the Armory for the Arts in the fall of 1982, just two months after it repeated its successful July "pillow concert" in September. Scandinavian women prepared food and the orchestra made some much needed money. The orchestra members fitted on the small stage of the Armory for the Arts because they were so few in number. Charitable comments suggested that the music was "over our heads." To quote Bob Wingert: "The Sibelius Second was a mistake—too complex a piece to attempt so early." Fortunately, no reviews of the concert seem to have survived.

Undaunted, the orchestra improved. Programs for the rest of the years were less ambitious (see Appendix I for a complete list of all SFCO programs), and the spring concert with June De Toth playing the Grieg Piano Concerto in A Minor was a resounding success. It was a performance that many players remember as a high point of the first season.

In addition to formal performances by the orchestra, a number of small groups from the orchestra performed in programs that supported worthwhile causes. Anne-Lise, in her *Short History,*[2] lists the following:

11/82: Concert in the Capitol Rotunda for the Governor and First Lady and government employees. The Governor presented the orchestra with a certificate "in appreciation for their generous contribution of time and talent."

11/82: Performance for the benefit of the Hadassah Women's Organization. A harp, string quartet, and woodwind quintet performed.

12/82: Two performances for students at Wood-Gormley Elementary School.

1/83: Performance for the entire student body at Alvord Elementary School.

2/83: Performance at the Museum of New Mexico for the opening of the Filigree Exhibit.

3/83: Concert in the Capitol Rotunda for the Governor and First Lady, the legislature, and government employees. A group from a Las Vegas institution was invited by Mrs. Anaya. Their reaction to what was to them an unusual treat was touching and rewarding. The orchestra was again awarded a certificate of "Appreciation and Recognition."

3/83: Performance for the Crime Stopper Benefit Carnival at Sweeney Center.

4/83: Performance for the entire student body at Capshaw Junior High School.

4/83: Performance for P.E.O. Sisterhood, Chapter P.S.F.N.M.

11/83: Concert for 400 students of Santa Fe schools at James A. Little Theater, New Mexico School for the Deaf.

The orchestra also sponsored a free music class at St. John's College every Saturday morning from 9:00 to 10:30.

This first year was an ambitious beginning which no doubt created an impetus for future success.

Governor's Award

Bob Wingert

Bob was just right for this fledgling group. He had everyone's respect for his knowledge and musicianship. He knew what life in a professional orchestra was like, but he could back off and appreciate that a community orchestra is made up of community musicians who play for a wide audience. Perhaps he was too easy-going, and discipline was sometimes a problem in rehearsals, but this inexperienced group of musicians wasn't ready for a field-marshal approach. His knowledge of string playing was minimal, and combined with his general demeanor, he had to depend on others to enforce bowing. Fortunately he could invite some of his professional orchestra colleagues to help with that task

Atmosphere

The term "informal" does not catch the vitality and openness of the young musicians who were the SFCO in the first few years. Stories abound, not all of which should become part of a public document. But a few follow:

A flute player couldn't figure out to whom Bob was talking when he addressed "celli"; she couldn't identify a "Shelly" in the cello section.

Peter Shoenfeld, a volunteer firefighter, would leave rehearsals when his "hooter" went off and come back dirty and smelling of smoke. In 1982 Santa Fe was one of the largest cities in the state to have only a volunteer fire department.

Pat Greathouse brought her young children with her—

Emily would lie under the chair with her blanket, sucking her thumb while the boys played in the hallway. Children were at rehearsals then more than today, though we've had Alex, Ted Vives's son, the last couple years.

In 1982, there was no youth symphony, so good teenagers played in the orchestra. And there were other "characters," a woman given a ride from a shelter, a drunk who had to be asked to leave, people who thought they were too good for the orchestra and ought to be paid.

But this was a younger group. People were dating each other and seeing each other. A group used to go to the Green Onion Tavern after rehearsal and have a few beers, Bob Wingert included. The core group that continued in the orchestra grew older together and the atmosphere became more staid.

So, with hard work, camaraderie, good leadership, enthusiastic support, and a welcoming environment, an orchestra was born.

**Santa Fe Community Orchestra, 1982,
Robert Wingert, Music Director**

3

MUSIC THROUGHOUT THE YEARS

A complete list of compositions performed in the formal concerts played in the orchestra's twenty-five years is provided in Appendix I. After a summary of compositions performed, some of the high points of those concerts will be noted in more detail.

A Summary

The orchestra played 90 concerts in its first 25 years. Some 63 composers were programmed, including 24 composers the first season.

For the most part the programming was traditional. Composers and the number of times scheduled were:

Mozart 26
Beethoven 17
Brahms 13
Bizet 8
Handel 6
Tchaikovsky 6

There were others that added interest to programs:

Barber 5
Copland 3
Janacek 3
Berg 3
Stravinsky 3

A few more adventurous composers:

Juan Antonio Arriaga y Balzola
William Bergsma
Zdenek Fibich
Vladas Jakubenas
Joseph Martin Kraus
Eduard Napravnik
Arvo Pärt
Stephen Paulus
Einojuhani Rautavaara
Erkki Salmenhaara
Heikki Suolahti
Tillman Susato

And premieres by

Christopher Berg
Richard Chrisiansen
James Medary Cooper
Jody Ellis
Gabriel Gonzales
Robert C. Jones
Joseph Martin Kraus
Heinz Marti
Jennifer McLaughlin
Gerald Near
Panaiotis
Steven Paxton
Erkki Salmenhaara

That's an enviable record for the first couple decades of a community orchestra!

Program Highlights

To choose program highlights from the rich 25-year history of concerts is a daunting task, and clearly shows the biases of the writer. Others might have chosen differently.

1982-83, The First Season

As noted previously, the orchestra attempted the Sibelius Second Symphony for the first concert; not a happy choice. But of interest on that program was Juan Antonio de Arriaga y Balzola's overture to his early nineteenth-century opera *Los esclavos felices*. In the spring Wingert programmed William Bergsma's music to the ballet *Paul Bunyan* (1937), a good start to diversified programming.

Members who played that first year remember the March 13 performance of Grieg's Piano Concerto in A Minor with soloist June De Toth as a high point. Ms. De Toth had studied in Rome and Salzburg, performed in Carnegie Hall and New York's Town Hall, and gave the first-ever all Bartók concert in New York City. It was, apparently a stunning performance to be remembered so well 25 years later.

1983-84

August brought another concert in the Palace of Governors, appropriately with Spanish music by Arriaga, Chabrier, and de Falla. The fall concert featured a Haydn Cello Concerto performed by Laurel Rogers. Laurel was one of several professional musicians who helped the orchestra in its early years; she played in the cello section for five concerts in addition to her concerto performance.

The spring concert featured Rosemarie Caminiti singing *Songs of a Wayfarer* (Mahler), and the Stravinsky *Suite pour Petit Orchestra (No 1)*. Newspaper articles in the early years announced the concerts, but there were few reviews. The second year continued varied and interesting programs.

1984-85

The year of the Sneetches. Bob Wingert remembered the Sneetches as a charming piece for children, and William Dunning wrote in the *New Mexican*:[3]

> Headlining their performance was a new work for children by local composer Stanley Lawrence, *The Sneetches*, a setting of the children's book by Dr. Seuss. Lawrence's work for narrator and orchestra featured Robert Saam reading the suave text. A variety of predictable orchestral sounds underlined the whimsy of the tale, with assorted sound effects, whistles and yells in place here and there. Robert Wingert conducts with enthusiasm and insight. His percussion section worked hard in this concert and is the best of the ensemble. The winds needed the most help. Between them rank the strings, with the low strings doing the better job.

Another professional musician, Lynn D. Case, performed the Mendelssohn Violin Concerto in E Minor, Op. 64, in the spring concert. And in July Ruben Romero performed his own composition, *Four Pieces for Guitar and Orchestra*, and the Vivaldi Concerto for Guitar. The program was coordinated with the first Santa Fe Guitar Festival. Also on the program, a Suzuki Children's String Ensemble performed a Vivaldi concerto.

Suzuki Student

In her first public appearance, 4-year-old Leah Wilson performed with other Suzuki students and the Santa Fe Community Orchestra for hundreds of music lovers in Cathedral Park.

It was a busy few months for soloists with the orchestra.

At the end of this second year, one might say the orchestra had found its stride. Three formal concerts a year, excellent soloists, interesting music, and overall improvement.

November 1985 began a close relationship with harpist Rosalind Simpson. In this concert she was joined by Shelby Boggio in Mozart's Concerto for Flute and Harp in C Major, K. 299. She performed as soloist an additional four times over the next twenty years as well as helped the orchestra from time to time with orchestral harp parts.

In a later review of a 1990 concert,[4] Craig Smith wrote about Rosalind Simpson:

> Harpist Rosalind Simpson was the assured guest soloist in Mario Castelnuovo-Tedesco's *Concerto for Harp and Orchestra*. What was especially nice about Simpson's work was her quiet competence and relaxed yet graceful stage presence. She is a *placid-appearing* performer, who never *plays* placidly. While not descending to mere flailing the instrument, she produces maximum tone with sensitive insight and firm technique. Simpson brought a widely colored palette to the *Concerto*, and her work in passages in harmonics in complicated solo and self-accompanied sections was exemplary.
>
> In a section in which the performer knocks in rhythm on the harp case with one hand while playing strings with other, imitating guitar rhythms, was charming
>
> The SFCO strings and winds accompanied with a will, and with more exactness of ensemble and accuracy than they had exhibited in the Handel.

The spring 1986 concert included Copland *Music from The Red Pony*, liked so well by the orchestra that it was repeated in 1997. Also on that program, Elaine Heltman was soloist in Marcello's Concerto in C Minor for Oboe and Strings. Elaine performed again in 1994 and, like Rosalind Simpson, helped the orchestra in the oboe section in six later concerts.

Bob Wingert stepped down briefly from the podium in the fall of 1986 to perform two pieces, a premiere of a piece by Jennifer McLaughlin, *Out for Clarinet and Orchestra,* and *Adagio* by Heinrich Baermann (but attributed to Richard Wagner). Bob's impressive and extensive credentials (a few: *Hochschule für Musik,* Vienna, Austria; Indiana University; Cleveland Institute; and experience in the Atlanta Symphony, the Santa Fe Symphony, and other orchestras), and obvious musical talent made him a favorite soloist with the orchestra. (A more complete description of Bob's credentials appears in a later section.)

The Shostakovich *Festival Overture* on the same program must have been a good test of the orchestra's increasing maturity, at least if taken up to its sometimes impossibly-fast tempo. We'll assume it was done well.

The only time Bob Wingert remembered stopping and starting over in a performance was in Bach's *Magnificat* in April 1987. Conductors remember episodes like that. The organ console being below stage left, string bass players inadvertently blocked the organist's view. The anxiety level of the whole orchestra goes up in such situations. Maya Hoffman was in the audience that day and was very complimentary; apparently the restart was done expeditiously. The Salmenhaara piece on that program was a surprise; Jack Briese got it in Helsinki when Finland was sponsoring composers and making music available at very low cost.

Bob Wingert also remembered Sandra Dudek-Twibell singing *Non più mesta accanto al fuoco* from Rossini's *La Cenerentola (Cinderella)* in April 1989. It was a great surprise, since she wasn't a well-known professional singer at that point. "She blew everyone away." She matched that performance with *Ozean, du Ungeheuer* from Weber's *Oberon,* and two Puccini arias in December 1993. Bob wasn't a fan of Broadway musicals, so the Stephen Sondheim piece from *Sweeney Todd* in the 1989 concert was a nice surprise.

Three other performers who would return later made their first appearance with the orchestra in this time period.

Joel and Beth Scott performed the Telemann Suite in F Major for Two Horns, Strings and Continuo in November 1987. They were professionals who played in all the major New Mexican orchestras over the course of their careers and returned to perform the Beethoven Sextet for Two Horns and Strings in June 1998. Joel has continued occasionally to sub in the community orchestra.

Ron Grinage performed the Chopin Piano Concerto No. 1 in E Minor in the fall of 1989. Craig Smith wrote in *The New Mexican:* [5] "Santa Fe pianist Grinage, making his local orchestral debut, proved capable of meeting and mastering both the extraverted and introverted demands of the formidable concerto, displaying both a confident command of the notes and a warm approach to the work as music." And, characteristically, Smith goes on: "Despite Wingert's valiant work and clear beat, the collaboration between orchestra and soloist through the concerto was at best brassy, and at worst watery and tentative. ....All in all, this concert was of quite respectable quality as a labor of love and as such deserved high marks."

In this first eight years the orchestra grew from a group of enthusiastic amateur musicians to one that Smith reviewed critically. The orchestra was an easy target for criticism, but the implication was that it was worth comparing to one of higher quality.

The orchestra experienced some first growing pains during this period. A quick inspection of the programs for the first eight years showed increasing complexity and the need to fill out all the sections of the orchestra. Pat Greathouse was the personnel manager those early years and spent hours recruiting players from as far afield as Albuquerque, Los Alamos, and Taos. Bob Wingert's reputation and the involvement of several of his professional friends were helpful in that effort.

Martha Dean Kerr, the orchestra's concertmaster for all of its early years, described difficulty in enforcing violin bowings. Discipline was not one of Wingert's strong points, and playing correct bowings, an imperative for professional orchestra string players, was foreign to many of the amateur string players in the orchestra. Martha's musical leadership, her cajoling, and the involvement of professionals assisting the orchestra were of some help, and over time things improved. The problem is endemic to amateur orchestras. The orchestra has made significant progress under Oliver Prezant's leadership.

1991-1997

Looking back over his tenure with the orchestra, Bob Wingert remembered Tom and Charmaine Weber playing Mozart's Concerto in C Major for Two Violins and Orchestra, K. 190, in April 1991. Charmaine had one of those really fast second violin parts that she played with amazing virtuosity.

The June 1991 concert featured two interesting pieces: Vladas Jakubenas's 1940 composition *Rapsodija* and Janacek's *Vlasske Tance*, Op. 2. The 1991-92 year was fairly traditional, though there was a sprinkling of unfamiliar composers' names, but the next year provided plenty of variety:

Marylinda Gutierrez played Concierto Andaluz, Op. 81 by Thomas de Hartmann; John Clark played a piece by Giuseppe Capuzzi, Concerto for Violone, for double bass; and Rosalind Simpson returned to play a concerto for harp by Karl Ditters von Dittersdorf. Dancer Lili del Castillo performed with the orchestra, for the first time, to music from *Carmen*. And there were pieces by Granados, Rodrigo, Turina, and McLaughlin (*The Distance of the Moon*), all in all a very interesting year.

Janice Felty, mezzo soprano, sang songs by Christopher Berg on both March and April concerts in 1993. Interesting titles: *A Lover's Cosmology and the Meaning of Hell,* and *From Not Waving but Drowning.* Sandra Twibell followed the next fall with selections from *Turandot, Tosca, and Oberon.*

In the spring of 1994 Kathleen MacIntosh and Elaine Heltman joined orchestra musicians Martha Dean Kerr and Tom Terwilliger to play the *Brandenburg Concerto No. 3.* Richard Hall, fresh from the Houston Symphony where he had his professional career, played a Vivaldi concerto for bassoon and joined Elaine for Paul Valjean's *Three Lyrics for Oboe, Bassoon & Strings.*

The orchestra has been fortunate to attract distinguished musicians to perform as soloists. In April 1995, Ruth Sommers, sister of orchestra clarinetist Allen Glasser, came out from New York to play the Haydn Concerto for Cello and Orchestra in C Major. In a complex cello section there was panic. Eventually it came back together. Sommers thought she was the problem and worried about performing again. Of course she went on to continue her distinguished solo career as well as direct the Festival Chamber Music organization in New York.

The fall of 1996 brought Theresa Coggeshall, soprano, to sing Barber's *Knoxville: Summer of 1915,* a piece she repeated in 2001. It was a stunning performance that many of us remember and were delighted when she repeated it. The text is based on James Agee's short story, was commissioned by soprano Eleanor Steber, and first performed by the Boston Symphony in 1948. Like the rest of us, Bob Wingert loved the piece and remembered the performance with pride and pleasure. I guess we all have recollections of lying on our back looking up at the stars on a summer night.

A distinguished member of the Santa Fe musical community, Maya Hoffman, performed the Chopin Piano Concerto No. 2 in 1996 and the Mozart Piano Concerto No. 24 in C Minor in 1998. Maya made her

Town Hall debut in 1956, and has performed internationally, including Wigmore Hall in London and the Concertgebouw in Amsterdam. She has performed numerous times in Santa Fe, where she is known as a champion and supporter of new music.

Contemporary composer Stephen Paulus's *Manhattan Serenade* was also on the 1996 program. Paulus was twice the composer-in-residence for the Santa Fe Chamber Music Festival.

And so with the end of the 1998 season, Bob Wingert's tenure as director of the orchestra also ended after 17 years, to the disappointment of all in the orchestra. One of his last concerts with the orchestra was a program at the Children's Museum, the orchestra's second appearance there and one Bob thought important in the effort to reach young children with good music and get them interested at an early age

His letter to the orchestra upon his departure is poignant but upbeat; to quote sections:

Dear SFCO Members:

This should be an exciting and interesting time for the orchestra. I have been offered some opportunities in Seattle which I feel I must take advantage of. I am therefore requesting from the orchestra a leave of absence for a year beginning this September. This will be a great opportunity for the orchestra to experience new leadership and different approaches. . . . The community is coming to expect a continuation of and improvement in the quality performances which they have seen through the years. In short, the orchestra is pursuing new channels and ways to improve. . . .

Trying a major change in one's life is always a difficult decision, especially when one is of such an advanced age as I am. I am very grateful to the orchestra for allowing me this opportunity to explore possibilities in a new climate. I plan to soak up a lot of humidity and will very likely need to come back to New Mexico to dry out. My sincerest thanks to all of you for your contributions to making great music and to making the SFCO such an enjoyable organization. I know your love of music will insure a continued commitment to and a bright future for the SFCO.

Most sincerely,
Robert Wingert

1998-2007

Wendy McGuire, the orchestra's timpanist, was president of the Board of Directors when Bob left, and so had the responsibility of leading the process to find a new director. Four prospective conductors were auditioned at a rehearsal, including Oliver Prezant. Oliver had substituted for Wingert at a rehearsal, and on the strength of those two exposures, Oliver was asked to conduct the fall 1998 concert; the Beethoven Symphony No. 1 was on the program. Based on good feedback from orchestra members, Oliver was asked to complete the season, and did so; Robert C. Jones conducted several soloist accompaniments on the spring concert.

Even from the start, Oliver worked on basic issues of ensemble—attacks and pitch primarily—an effort augmented by workshops, such as Playing in Tune, and increasingly frequent and well-attended sectionals, primarily for strings.

The orchestra worked hard in the 1998-99 year. In addition to three formal concerts, and, with the help of the Greater Access Program of the Santa Fe Arts Commission, the orchestra performed four neighborhood concerts targeted to children, one in St. Francis Auditorium and three in neighborhood elementary schools.

The first workshop of the year was at Nava Elementary School. Wendy McGuire explained how to make a simple string instrument using a bleach bottle, some fishing line, a strip of wood, and some screw eyes.

One young woman even got to conduct the orchestra, with just a little help from Oliver Prezant.

Making "Instruments"

Guest Conductor (Photographs by James Klebau)

Another workshop for children took place at Larragoite Elementary School in Santa Fe in 1989. Children were invited to come an hour before the orchestra's neighborhood concert, to make instruments out of various household materials (flower pots, paper cups, string, etc.). The big project was to make tom-toms from flower pots covered with rubber (roof membrane) that was secured and stretched with cord.

Robert C. Jones, composer, and a member of the orchestra, wrote a simple piece for the children to play with the orchestra. Here he's instructing his young musicians about when to play.

We all learned that year how good Oliver Prezant is with children, engaging them in the music, explaining how instruments work, leading them to make music of their own. The orchestra played many programs for children over the next ten years, often using music to be performed on an upcoming formal concert, to which one and all were invited.

Robert Jones Directs His Student Orchestra

During the 1998-1999 year of children's workshops, violinist Elena Sopoci (*Zigeunerweisen* and *The Lark Ascending*) and trumpeter Greg Heltman (Hummel Concerto) were soloists both in formal concerts and events for children. Orchestra members Britt Ravnan and Tom Terwilliger were soloists in the June concert.

In Oliver Prezant's first year as director, 1999-2000, the orchestra added a fourth concert to its season. In retrospect it was a fairly easy year, though to many adding a fourth concert seemed too heavy a burden—but it worked. Quoting Oliver, Craig Smith wrote[6] "I think getting people to have a better quality of musical experience is always the goal of working with musicians," Prezant said about his hopes for the group. "And bringing music to the audiences so that they have a real involvement with the score." "Rather than 'a better quality of musical experience,' I would say a deeper involvement with the music." Prezant noted that lecturing is similar to directing. "With an orchestra, it's more hands-on with respect to the music itself," he said. "With an audience, you're really talking about the way people hear. But it's important for an orchestra to listen and hear too." "Conducting is a little mysterious," Prezant said. "You don't make the sound yourself; you only make the sound with the orchestra. Whatever happened in rehearsal is just a point of reference when you're all onstage together. It's all about getting to know one another and getting to know the music."

Mary Ann Martinez, flutist and original member of the orchestra, performed as soloist twice that year: Henrik Andressen's *Variations on a Theme by Couperin* (with harpist Rosalind Simpson), and a Vivaldi Concerto for Flute and Strings. A high point for the orchestra, and an interesting piece that we played well, was Einojuhani Rautavaara's *Cantus Articus, Concerto for Birds and Orchestra*, Op. 61. There were also *Fanfares—for the Common Man* (Aaron Copland),—*for the Common Cold* (P.D.Q Bach),—and *for the Uncommon Woman* (Joan

Tower). Kelvin McNeal played Gershwin's *Rhapsody in Blue*; he would in 2003 return to play the Rachmaninoff Piano Concerto No. 2. We were off the ground with a new conductor.

Robert C. Jones, a clarinetist in the orchestra, played his own composition in October 2000, *Prelude, Air and Capriccio for Alto Saxophone and Chamber Orchestra*. The most interesting programming for the 2000-2001 season was in February, when the program was devoted to Romeo and Juliet—Berlioz, Prokofiev, Tchaikovsky, and Bernstein (*Symphonic Dances from West Side Story*). Theater Grottesco performed during the playing of the Berlioz *Romeo and Juliet*, not an easy venue given the sight lines in St. Francis Auditorium. The Prokofiev suite was another of those high points that orchestra members remember. Commenting on the Bernstein *Dances*, Oliver Prezant wrote:[7]

> The orchestra was sometimes playing "scared" when we took on a challenge that was big for us at the time, like the *Symphonic Dances from West Side Story*. Everyone was relieved, and when we got through it, that became a reference point and a stepping stone. There were many breakthroughs along the way, and there are more to come, I'm sure. In general, people have more confidence in the process and in their own ability at this point.

On sabbatical from the Paris Opera, Veronique Marcel arrived in Santa Fe in 1999 to collaborate with American performers and further expand her musical horizons. She graciously performed the Sibelius Violin Concerto, Op. 47, with the orchestra in April 2000.

Oliver continued the tradition of a competition within the orchestra for members who wanted to perform as soloists with the orchestra. Those selected played entire compositions or, in some cases, one or two movements. Over the course of the next seven years, the soloists were the following:

June 2001:
> James Knudson, cello / Saint-Saens, *Cello Concert No. 1, Op. 33*

April 2002:
> Michael Ebinger, trumpet / Hovhaness, *Prayer of St. Gregory*

October 2002:
> Gerald Fried, oboe; Michael Golden, clarinet; Elizabeth Hunke, horn; James Preus, bassoon / Mozart, *Sinfonia Concertante*

> Gerald Fried, oboe / Fried, *Time Travel for Oboe and Orchestra*

December 2003:
> James Preus, clarinet / Debussy, *Premiere Rhapsodie*

> Debra Poulin, bassoon / Vivaldi, *Concerto No. 7*

April 2005:
> Stuart Bloom, percussion / Milhaud, *Concerto for Percussion and Chamber Orchestra*

> Steven Ovitsky, horn / Mozart, *Concerto No. 3 in E flat for Horn, K. 447*

April 2006:
> Gerald Fried, oboe / Cimarosa, *Concerto for Oboe and Strings*

> Dina Matz, cello / Dvorak, *Concerto for Cello and Orchestra,* Adagio movement

The orchestra started the October 2001 concert, a month after the 9/11 tragedy, with *America the Beautiful*, and then played the Largo from the Dvorak *New World Symphony*. If music can elicit strong emotions, it did so on that day, for both audience and orchestra members.

In March 2002 the orchestra embarked on the first of three large choral works to be performed over the next several years. They were all very successful, and Oliver Prezant worked very hard behind the scenes to recruit and rehearse soloists and chorus members, for the choruses in these large works were composed of members of various choral groups in the community.

March 10, 2002:

Beethoven's Symphony No. 9. Soloists were Louise Mendius, Tim Willson, Consuelo Sanudo, and Loren Jacobson. The performance was at Santa Maria de la Paz Catholic Community. Choristers included members of the following choral groups: Coro de Cámara, the Santa Fe Men's Camerata, the Zia Singers, The College of Santa Fe Chorus and members of the community. To quote Oliver[7] describing the concert:

> The performance of Beethoven's Ninth in 2002 was an extraordinary experience for all involved. It was a few months after 9/11, my students from the College of Santa Fe, who had not been able to sing a simple Palestrina *Sanctus* in the key of F the semester before, had finally learned the double fugue in the finale, and the violins had had an extra nine hours of work on the music in sectionals, some of which were focused on playing F# in tune in the key of D major. We had

our biggest audience to that point, in Santa Maria de la Paz church. I had been wondering whether we could find soloists for the piece, and had been dragging my feet about whether to change the program, when miraculously, Tim Willson, a fine tenor from the Metropolitan Opera chorus, retired to Santa Fe just in time. By the time we got to the fourth movement and the chorus stood and the baritone sang, the concert had taken on a life of its own... By the end of the piece, the response was overwhelming. People really needed to hear that piece of music just then. The orchestra, the chorus, and the soloists rose to the occasion, and while it was not a technically perfect performance, one of the orchestra members, a very experienced professional musician, said, "that was a great performance, by any standard." Of course, it was the feeling that he was talking about. And you can hear it in the recording. There's an energy, openness, and a spirit to it that you can feel from beginning to end. The next week, when I was away, a good part of the rehearsal was devoted to orchestra members talking about the experience of playing that piece in that performance and how much it meant to them.

March 7, 2004:

Orff's *Carmina Burana*. Soloists were Joanna Morska-Osinska, Kent Wall, and Brian Podolny. Performance was at the Sweeney Center. The chorus included members of the community, singers from numerous local choral groups, and The College of Santa Fe. Again, quoting Oliver:[7]

Of course, the big choral performances have all been very special. There's so much going on during the performance that sometimes it's hard to maintain a perspective. But someone that I knew well came backstage after *Carmina Burana* looking absolutely shaken after hearing the last number, and it was clear that she had been deeply affected by the performance. People love the fact that they can come to a concert and see their friends and neighbors deeply involved in the performance. They are rooting for the orchestra, and they're not looking for superficial perfection, and it means they get involved with the performance in a different way.

March 5, 2006:

Verdi's *Requiem*. Soloists were Marilyn Barnes, Monika Renée Cosson-Sheppard, Andre Garcia-Nuthmann, and Frederick Fox. Performance was at Santa Maria de la Paz Catholic Community. Once again the chorus included members of the community, singers from numerous local choral groups, and the College of Santa Fe.

These were big events with hundreds of participants and large and enthusiastic audiences, and might be considered a "reach" for a community orchestra in a small town. They were successful and satisfying to orchestra members. It's too bad that no reviews are available.

The June 2002 concert was Spanish and Mariachi. After *Iberia*, by Albeniz, and Rosalind Simpson playing a Ginastera Concerto for Harp and Orchestra, the Mariachi El Tigre took over.

Mr. Antonio Mendoza

They played several traditional mariachi numbers, including *Santa Fe, La Reyna* (Santa Fe, the Queen), composed by Mr. Antonio Mendoza for the occasion.

Beginning in the 2002-2003 season, the orchestra, with grant money from the Mill Atelier Foundation, made programs available to give New Mexico composers a venue for their compositions. Some compositions were programmed on regular concerts, and others on special concerts titled *New Works by New Mexico Composers*. As a sample, the following compositions by orchestra members have been performed on two concerts featuring music by SFCO composers:

Jody Ellis / *The Ancient Ones (Anasazi); The Dreams of Kokopelli*

Gerald Fried / *Time Travel for Oboe and Orchestra; the Roots Suite*

Robert C. Jones / *Four Symphonic Images; Chaconne à son Goût, Orchestra Variations on 'L 'Homme Armee'*

Ted Vives / *Introduction and Overture; Children's Suite*

John Michael Luther / *Costa del Sol Overture*

And this does not do justice to all the compositions performed on evenings dedicated to readings of *New Works by New Mexico Composers.*

Two stunning solo performances in the past two years were Margaret Carpenter playing the Prokofiev *Violin Concerto No. 2,* and Amanda Pepping playing the Hummel *Trumpet Concerto in E Major* (and some virtuoso trumpet solos). The concert with Amanda Pepping was the first concert the SFCO played in the Lensic Performing Arts Center.

Mariachi Performers

Orchestra Buddies

Howard Pakin, a horn player in the orchestra, got the idea for the Orchestra Buddy program after watching children in the audience at a Santa Fe Children's Museum concert.

The Buddy program brought children aged 9-12 into rehearsals to provide them with up-close and personal experience with orchestra instruments and musicians. Buddies helped with routine rehearsal tasks, setting up chairs and distributing music, for example. Then they were free to roam through the orchestra and observe how an orchestra makes music.

Gussie Fauntleroy wrote an article in the *New Mexican* describing the program:[8]

> Each Buddy is taken under the wing of an orchestra member who introduces the child around and answers any questions they may have. Each child also receives a T-shirt proclaiming, "I am a Santa Fe Community Orchestra Orchestra Buddy." . . .

> It was a natural for Colton Ratcliffe, a third-grader at the Waldorf School, to become an Orchestra Buddy. He had already started attending rehearsals at the invitation of his cello teacher, Jody Ellis.

> At the time, Colton had played the cello for about a year. His interest in the instrument was sparked when he saw Ellis perform with the Santa Fe Community Orchestra at a concert for children...

> "One of the best things about the program is there's really nothing to do, other than assign someone to answer [the Buddy's] questions and make them feel part of the group," he said. "The kids win, the community wins, the fine arts group wins."

Jody Ellis and Colton Ratcliffe

Let's Dance!

Let's Dance! was a new adventure for the orchestra in 2005, one that required prodigious effort on the part of orchestra members to make it succeed.

Unaccustomed as many were to playing "pop" music, nevertheless the orchestra played show tunes, waltzes, and other program music fairly well.

The Great Big Jazz Band joined in alternating sets, with Robert C. (Bob) Jones leading that group. In fact, Eddie Daniels, a noted clarinetist, and Jerry Weimer, a student at the College of Santa Fe, put in guest appearances to improvise with the band. Ron Grinage, a long-time pianist at the Cantina at La Casa Sena, played a medley of 14 Gershwin tunes arranged by SFCO clarinetist Robert C. Jones; a few other arrangements were provided by SFCO member Ted Vives.

2004 - 2005 Concert Season

The Santa Fe Community Orchestra
Oliver Prezant ◆ Music Director

Let's Dance!

An Evening of Swing and
Ballroom Dancing
Featuring The SFCO &
The Santa Fe Great Big Jazz Band
with
Ron Grinage and Special Guests

Let's Eat!
Dinner & Cash Bar
The Cowgirl Hall of Fame

Friday, March 4th 7 - 10 pm
Sweeney Convention Center

This and other SFCO projects made possible in part by New Mexico Arts, a division of the Office of Cultural Affairs, and the National Endowment for the Arts; the Santa Fe Arts Commission and the 1% Lodger's Tax.

Let's Dance

Audience and orchestra reaction to the first event was overwhelmingly positive. The 400-seat hall was filled from the moment the doors opened. Catering was provided by the Cowgirl Restaurant, and everyone, from the audience to the orchestra, right down to the security guards had a great time and asked when we would be doing the event again. The opportunity to dance to a live orchestra and a big band brought out the dance community, and many enjoyed the atmosphere of a wedding reception with no bride and groom.

The event was repeated the next year at the Eldorado Hotel, sponsored by St. Vincent Hospital, Sweeney Center by that time being under reconstruction. Chris Calloway was the featured vocalist the second year. Added to the program was a silent auction that took untold hours to organize, the result of which was a significant cash benefit for the orchestra. Janet Steinberg, a violinist with the SFCO, provided capable leadership of a volunteer committee for the 2006 effort.

Resources

The reader will certainly have developed the impression from the description of recent activities that the program of the orchestra was expanding significantly in the most recent decade, and that has been the case. Resources have kept up with expenses, and both have increased dramatically. In the first half of the orchestra's life, expenses were less than $15,000 per year; in the second half, resources and expenses increased dramatically to approximately $50,000 in the 2007 fiscal year.

This is, of course, due in large part to the efforts of dedicated orchestra members and volunteers who work on grant proposals.

4

MUSICIANS

Over the course of the 25 years of the orchestra's existence, 558 musicians have performed with the orchestra. However, of note, three-fourths, or 441 of them played fewer than 10 concerts. Some of the 441 were professionals who came in to help, and of course people come and go for all sorts of reasons unrelated to the musical experience they have in the orchestra, but even so, the impression is that a core of musicians has provided the continuity to keep the orchestra a vital musical organization in Santa Fe. Currently, some 65 members play more or less regularly with the orchestra. Orchestra members pay dues, and some are regular donors in addition to payment of their dues.

The orchestra is its members. Who are they; what are their characteristics? From recent surveys (51 members returned the survey):

None are younger than 18, and 14 are older than 64.
Men outnumber women 29 to 20.
Half live in the city (26), many (17) in the county, and a few commute from Los Alamos (4), Española, and Taos.
All but two are Caucasian; the two are Hispanic and Pacific Islander.
Many players support the orchestra in addition to playing their instruments; 5 have been president of the Board of Directors and 17 have served on the board. Four have written grants, and others have served as counsel, librarian, treasurer, and program annotator.

Members of the Santa Fe Community Orchestra are integral members of the community, as demonstrated by their occupations:[9]

Artist	Music Teacher
Artist/Gallery Owner	Musician/Composer
Attorney	N.M. State Government Administrator
Biochemist	Nonprofit Consultant
Book Store Owner	Nuclear Engineer
Bookkeeper/Retail Sales	Ophthalmologist
Broker Assistant	Paralegal
Business Entrepreneur	Pediatrician
Cello Teacher	Photographer
Classical/Jazz Musician	Physician
Composer	Physicist
Counselor/Therapist	Poet
Development Associate	Psychologist
Ecologist	Registered Nurse
Electrical Engineer	Retail Sales
Finance	School Administrator
Fire Ecologist	School Teacher
Geneticist	Social Scientist
Geologist	Software Engineer
Historian	Soil Scientist
Industrial Hygienist	Student
Investor	Teacher/Composer
Landscaper	Teacher/Journalist
Language/Music Teacher	Technical Writer
Luthier	Vision Scientist
Molecular Biologist	Wildlife Ecologist
Music Director	Writer

The employers of orchestra musicians are what one would expect from a glance at the list of occupations:

Educational institutions: 11, of which 7 were higher-education institutions

Science organizations: 9, of which 6 are the Los Alamos National Laboratory

Self-employed: 8

Legal firms: 3

Arts and music: 5, of which 2 are musicians in professional symphony orchestras and one a successful composer

Other: including military, religious institutions, publishing, and nonprofits

The musicians brought to the community orchestra a wide variety of experiences in previous musical groups:

Community bands and orchestras: 21

College orchestras: 15

Professional orchestras: 16; three players were members of six major professional orchestras, and 13 others listed professional and semi-professional orchestras.

Other: 11 Total

Organized chamber music groups: 1	Early music groups: 2
Festivals: 3	Folk/country: 1
Choral: 2	Jazz groups: 2

And they are active in other Santa Fe music groups:

Professional groups: 5, including Santa Fe Symphony (2), Santa Fe Pro Musica, Music de Camera, Santa Fe Concert Association Orchestra

Los Alamos Symphony: 4

Los Alamos Winds: 1

Santa Fe Concert Band: 5

Chamber music groups: 10, including string quartets (6), woodwind quintets (3), saxophone quartet

Other music groups: 14, including Jazz (6), mariachi (2), choral (3), Kammermusiks (1), N.M. Highlands, and Waldorf school music teachers

Our Music Directors

Robert Wingert

Robert was Director from 1982-1998. Some information from his résumé:

Robert began his studies as a scholarship student at the Cleveland Institute of Music, where he received a Bachelor of Music, with honors in clarinet, in 1963. In 1962, while at the Cleveland Institute, he attended the Berkshire Festival School of the Boston Symphony (Tanglewood).

His studies were interrupted by service in the United States Military Academy Band, West Point, N.Y., 1963-1966. After the army, he attended Indiana University, Bloomington, where he earned a Master of Music with distinction in clarinet (conducting minor), and also a Performer's Certificate (1967).

His first professional position was in the Atlanta Symphony Orchestra, Robert Shaw, Conductor, Second Clarinetist, 1967-1975. During his time in Atlanta, he found opportunities to attend the Blossom Festival School of the Cleveland Orchestra, 1968 and 1969, and the *Hochschule für Musik*, Vienna, Austria, where he did post-graduate study in clarinet and chamber music. 1973-1974, 1975-1977. When he was in Vienna after 1975, he had a substitute position, January-September 1977, as solo clarinetist in the *Sinfonie-Orchester des Suedwestfunks*, Baden-Baden, Germany, Ernest Bour, Conductor; and also substituted in the Vienna State Opera orchestra.

He moved to Santa Fe to play in the Santa Fe Opera,

second clarinetist, 1978 (substitute); extra clarinet, 1981, 1984, 1988, 1989; and later as principal clarinetist in the Santa Fe Symphony, 1984-1998, and principal clarinetist for Opera Southwest, 1985-1989, 1995-1998.

His awards include the Mayor's Award for "outstanding contribution to the development and enrichment of the arts in Santa Fe," 1990, and previously the Anne Gannett Award for Veterans, National Federation of Music Clubs, 1974, and an NDEA Title IV Fellowship at Indiana University, 1966-1967.

Robert Wingert

Winner 1990

The Mayor's Recognition Award for Excellence in the Arts

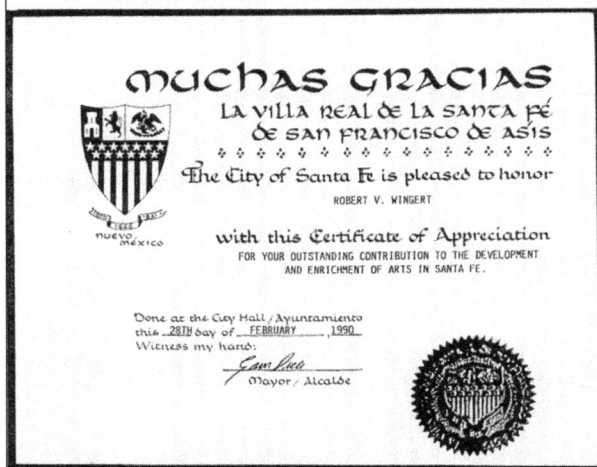

MUCHAS GRACIAS

LA VILLA REAL DE LA SANTA FÉ
DE SAN FRANCISCO DE ASÍS

❖ ❖ ❖ ❖ ❖ ❖ ❖ ❖ ❖ ❖ ❖ ❖ ❖ ❖ ❖ ❖

The City of Santa Fe is pleased to honor

ROBERT V. WINGERT

with this Certificate of Appreciation

FOR YOUR OUTSTANDING CONTRIBUTION TO THE DEVELOPMENT
AND ENRICHMENT OF ARTS IN SANTA FE.

Done at the City Hall / Ayuntamiento
this 28TH day of FEBRUARY , 1990
Witness my hand:

Mayor / Alcalde

1990, Mayor's Recognition Award

Oliver Prezant

Oliver Prezant studied conducting with Charles Bruck at the Pierre Monteux School, and also with Gurer Aykal and David Gilbert. As a violist, he has performed with the New Mexico Symphony Orchestra, the Santa Fe Opera, and the California Chamber Virtuosi. He was the viola soloist in the Santa Fe Stages production of Peter Brook's *Carmen*, and the principal violist on the national tour of Sondheim's *Into the Woods*. He was the recipient of a fellowship from the National Orchestral Association and holds a degree from the Mannes College of Music in New York City. He was the conductor of the Santa Fe Youth Symphony and has been a program director and conductor for the American Festival for the Arts in Houston.

As an educator, Mr. Prezant has presented lectures and educational programs for the Santa Fe Opera, the Santa Fe Chamber Music Festival, 20th Century Unlimited, the City of Santa Fe's *ArtWorks* program, the New Mexico Endowment for the Humanities, the College of Santa Fe, Elderhostel, Renesan, and the Tanglewood Association of Volunteers at the Berkshire Museum. He is the creator of *The Art of Listening*, a three-part introduction to classical music. Other workshop and presentation topics have included *Drama and Interaction for Musicians, Playing in Tune/Singing in Tune*, and *Elements of a Meaningful Arts Program*. He was the host of the Santa Fe Chamber Music Festival's radio show *Festival Insights* and has written and produced preview CDs for the Santa Fe Opera. His unique presentations for concert audiences, children and families, educators, school groups, and others have helped thousands of music-lovers deepen their appreciation and understanding of music. Mr. Prezant is currently an assistant professor in the Contemporary Music Program at the College of Santa Fe.

St. Francis Auditorium, 2005, Oliver Prezant, Music Director

The Players

Appendix II is a list of all the musicians who have played in the orchestra. So many of them have stories to tell; and so many should be recognized for their contributions. A few who have played the most concerts, were there at the start, and/or who made significant contributions are described here.

Mary Ann Martinez

Mary Ann Martinez, principal flute, played the first season and missed only two rehearsals in the next 25 years. Born in Embudo, Mary Ann grew up in Taos and Santa Fe. After graduating from the

University of New Mexico, with a minor in applied music (a student of Frank Bowen), she began a 35-year career teaching fourth grade at E.J. Martinez and Wood-Gormley elementary schools. After a brief retirement, she is again (2007) back in the classroom teaching ESL and Shelter English at Capshaw Middle School.

Mary Ann Martinez

Mary Ann's musical associations are many; she has performed with chamber ensembles in Santa Fe, Albuquerque, Los Alamos, and Acequipa, Peru; the Los Alamos Symphony; Los Alamos Choral Society; Chamisa Players; Aeolian Quintet; Kammermusik Chamber Orchestra; and the Albuquerque Symphony Orchestra.

As well as serving SFCO as section leader, Mary Ann has performed the Andriessen *Variations on a Theme by Couperin* Duo Concerto and the Vivaldi *Il Cardinello* Concerto with the orchestra. She served on the orchestra's board of directors and as grants administrator. She is currently flutist for the Cathedral Basilica of Saint Francis and performs with the Chugwater Piano Trio. In 2007, she performed in pick-up orchestras for *Palimpsest* for the Santa Fe Opera and *Strike the World* for St. John's College.

Jody Ellis

Newcomers to the orchestra know Jody Ellis as that lady with the lucky socks who, before each concert, leaves her seat in the cello section to warm up the audience. She's also the first to greet new members of the orchestra. But Jody is much more than that, along with Anne-Lise Cohen, a founder of the orchestra; a composer; and throughout its 25 years, a major player in the administration, organization, publicity, and operation of the orchestra.

Jody Ellis[14]

She's also a very attractive subject to those who write about the orchestra. In 2005, Kay Lockridge, in the *Santa Fe New Mexican*,[10] wrote:

> Some people study history. Others live it. And a few actually help create it. This is a story about one of those who has done all three over the past 50 years in Santa Fe.
>
> When Jody Ellis returned to Santa Fe in 1953 after serving as an Air Force nurse in Germany during the Korean War, she had no idea of the adventures that awaited her in the City Different.
>
> Now, more than 50 years later, Ellis marvels at the changes that have occurred in Santa Fe and her life, and she's looking forward, as usual, to the future. Yet, looking back to 1946 when she first arrived in Santa Fe, she said she "knew from the first time I stepped foot in the city that this was where I wanted to be forever."
>
> In the 25 years that followed her return to Santa Fe, Jody owned a candy store, worked as a secretary, worked in real estate, ran a consulting service for writers, and founded a quarterly literary magazine and, along with Marcia Muth, a publishing company, Sunstone Press.

Continuing the Lockridge article:

> Then began the love of Ellis' life, when she began playing the cello in 1979 and co-founded the Santa Fe Community Orchestra in which she plays to this day. Her musical career took a new path in 1985 when she broke her wrist, which hindered her playing in the orchestra for a while, so she turned to teaching the instrument to both children and adults. Ellis

specializes in helping adults with hand problems who want to play the cello and loves working with children. In recent years, she has turned her attention to composition of orchestral and piano music.

Jody Ellis, Composer

"In life, there are leaders and servers or helpers. I've always felt I was a server," Ellis suggests. To that end, she wrote a book, *The ABCs of Successful Living*, which was published more than 30 years ago and has just been re-issued by Sunstone Press as *Successful Living from A to Z*. In it, she expresses the philosophy that has guided her life: "Everyone can do something. You just need to find it and let it grow. If it's not fun, don't do it." Looking back over her 80 years of life, Ellis agrees that "it's been one heck of a ride, and it's not over yet."

Willard Chilcott

Willard Chillcott was a special member of the "can-do" folks in the early years of the orchestra. He didn't like playing his cello on the bare ground for the first two pillow concerts in 1982, so for the similar concerts in 1983 he built a stage (4' x 8' plywood set on supports) by himself and set it up in the Palace of Governors courtyard prior to the concerts. Then, when the orchestra started playing in St. Francis Auditorium, he took on still a larger challenge. The stage was too small and there was no place for the huge Bechstein grand piano the chamber music program had purchased. Phil Register, long-time architect, made drawings and got appropriate permissions, and Willard built new stage sections in his garage, figured out how to move the organ console, repositioned the carvings and spindles; the result: the new stage extension still an integral part of St. Francis Auditorium. The plaque on the front of the stage acknowledges the contribution of the community orchestra.

Willard Chilcott

Peter Shoenfeld

Peter Shoenfeld was an original member of the orchestra and has played 75 of the 90 concerts in the past 25 years. Peter is a distinguished attorney in Santa Fe, specializing in water issues. Asked about his leadership positions with the orchestra, he responded: "board member, counsel, incorporator, truck driver." We've all been brought back to the matter at hand by his humor and incisive wit.

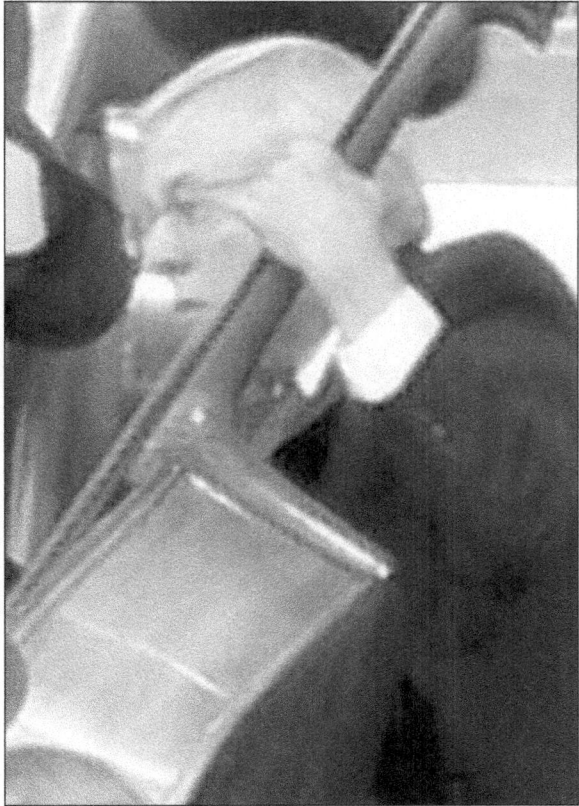

Peter Shoenfeld[14]

Martha Dean Kerr

Martha Dean Kerr played one concert the first year, and then played 69 more as concertmaster until 2003, when she moved away from Santa Fe. In 1982 she met Jody Ellis at the temple, where they both played. Jody suggested she audition. She did so, with Bob Wingert and others, and was asked to be concertmaster, which astonished her. She agreed.

Interviewed in 2007, she recounted 40 years of involvement in teaching instrumental and choral music, and particularly 18 years of teaching the Suzuki violin method in Santa Fe. Martha's passion was teaching young children—teaching them the violin and music. Speaking about a concert at the Children's Museum, she said "children listen intently and get excited by our music. Many of them will stand up and spontaneously tell us how they can play the violin too. We encourage them to ask questions."

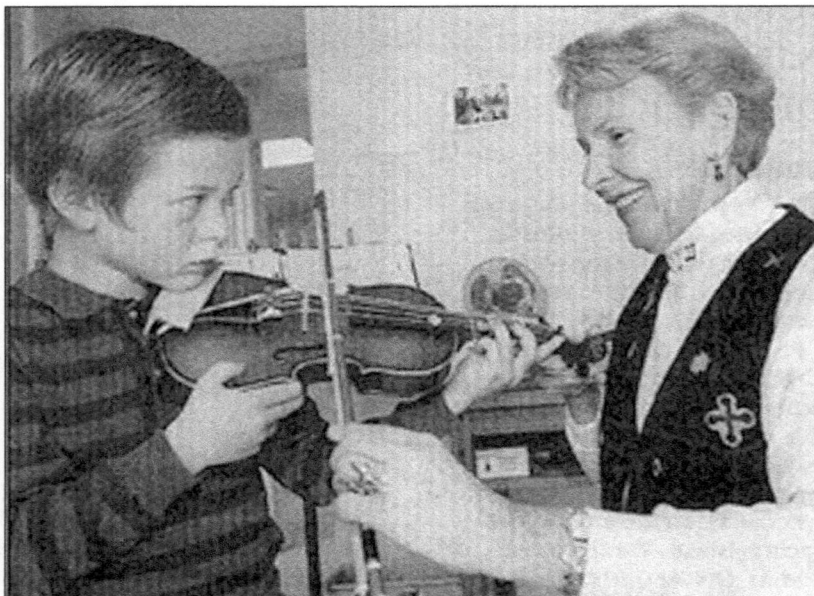

Martha Dean Kerr

Being a concertmaster of a volunteer orchestra brings challenges. The dynamics of who plays where in the section must be dealt with, and amateur violinists do not always see the importance of taking the concertmaster's bowings. Martha went about her responsibilities quietly and persistently. She generously led the way when an experiment to rotate members through the two violin sections met with some resistance. All in all, everyone liked and respected Martha as she performed that important role.

Marylinda Gutierrez

Marylinda Gutierrez joined the orchestra in 1984 and has been a steady member of the flute section, except for a couple years when she lived in Colorado. As noted earlier, she was Bernard Rubenstein's flutist in the first Santa Fe Symphony in the 1960s and has been a major contributor to music in the Santa Fe Public Schools as choir director during which she won the New Mexico Music Educators Association award and superior ratings for her choirs. She played the *Concierto Andaluz*, Op. 81, by Thomas de Hartmann, with the orchestra in 1992.

Marylinda Gutierrez[14]

Michael Golden

Michael Golden was an original member of the orchestra in 1982 and has been the principal clarinetist through most of the subsequent years. Michael is a family-law attorney and mediator in Santa Fe. He has experience in choral music (New York Collegiate Chorale, Chorus of Santa Fe) and played in the Taos Community Orchestra as well as chamber groups in Santa Fe.

Michael Golden[14]

Harold Geller

Harold Geller was an original member of the orchestra and has played 78 concerts since that time. He commutes from Taos, sometimes four days in a row, to play rehearsals and concerts. Harold was founder, and is currently board member of Music from Angel Fire, an annual nationally recognized chamber music festival, comprising world-class musicians, primarily from the Chamber Music Society, Lincoln Center, New York, now in its 24th season. He has owned the Total Arts Gallery in Taos since 1969.

Harold Geller[14]

Others

There are so many. *Donald Vasquez*, an original member, returned in 1998 after stays in Los Alamos and Albuquerque, during which he played in community orchestras. *Pat Greathouse* likewise took a sabbatical to raise a family and teach at Santa Fe Prep; she was personnel director in early years of the orchestra, directed Mozart y Mariachi, a violin education program in the Santa Fe Public Schools, and played in a mariachi group. Now, besides writing food reviews for the *New Mexican*, she's in the process of writing a book on the history of mariachi music. *Lisa Van Sickle* is a special person; she has done just about every job in support of the orchestra, including librarian, board member, vice president and president, grant writer, manager, et cetera. *Wendy McGuire* was president of the board during a difficult period; since retiring from the orchestra she has fulfilled her role as the Turkey Lady. A piece about her in the *New Mexican*[11] written by Pat Greathouse described her new pursuit. And there are many others who have contributed time and resources, as well as talent, to the orchestra. Appendix 2 lists all the musicians who have played with the orchestra.

Distinguished Musicians

Over the course of its twenty-five years, three professional musicians of national reputation have played with the orchestra.

Joe Mondragon:

When Peter Shoenfeld was 11 years old he had an album by Art Pepper on which Joe Mondragon was the bass player, and his name appeared on other albums. Mondragon came to Peter for legal help with a land title issue. Peter persuaded him to play in the orchestra, even though he had retired, He did so, bringing the largest double bass Peter had ever seen. The second time, he came back with a tiny double bass. Peter described him as a grizzled veteran.

John DiJanni:

John DiJanni took over the post of principal violist in the Metropolitan Opera Orchestra from his father in 1931. He knew he had arrived when, a couple years later, and after playing the solo viola part in a Wagner opera, his father leaned over and said "Nice job, Johnny." He could talk for hours about world-famous conductors and singers he had known. In the early years, he was very helpful to Bob Wingert in working with the orchestra's string players. He was a vital force in Santa Fe music for many years after he retired and moved here in the '60s.

Gerald Fried:

The current star of the orchestra is oboist Gerry Fried, who has played since shortly after moving to Santa Fe in 2000. After graduating from Juilliard in 1948, Gerry played oboe and English horn for eleven years with the Dallas Symphony, Pittsburgh Symphony, New York's Little Orchestra Society, and the Los Angeles Philharmonic. He then started a distinguished career as composer of music for films, television, and the stage. His credits as composer/conductor/orchestrator fill seven single-spaced pages, including an Emmy award for Best Score for the television program *Roots*, scores for the first five Stanley Kubrick movies, including *Paths of Glory*, and an Oscar nomination for Best Score for a movie. He has been a member of the Executive Committee of the Academy of Motion Picture Arts and Sciences since 1968. More recently *The Chess Game* (inspired by *Alice in Wonderland*) was premiered by the New York Bargemusic Festival; and *Rock of Angels*, a bluegrass opera, was performed by Pro Musica in 2006 in Santa Fe. One could write pages about his awards and credits; the samples provided here give some impression of the breadth and quality of this wonderful musician.

Gerald Fried

CHAPTER 5

EXPANSION OF THE ORCHESTRA'S PROGRAM

Mission

SFCO Mission Statement / September 2006

The mission of the Santa Fe Community Orchestra is to provide an opportunity for volunteer musicians to perform free orchestral concerts for a broad range of Santa Fe and Northern New Mexico audiences, to present free educational programs for audiences of all ages, to engage New Mexico musicians as soloists, to promote the composition and performance of works by New Mexico composers, and to support the musical and cultural life of Santa Fe.

The orchestra has grown in many ways during the nine years of Oliver Prezant's leadership. His view of the nature of a community orchestra, and the Board of Directors' support of that view, have determined the direction of that growth. One important purpose of a community orchestra is to provide a valuable musical experience for the players, a view shared by Oliver and all those interviewed for this book. The essential components of that "valuable musical experience" are quality and diversity. Following in this section are examples of activities designed to improve quality, and of program initiatives (e. g., theme concerts, new works by New Mexico composers, commissioning) to increase diversity of musicians' experiences.

Five Concerts

Prior to Oliver Prezant's appointment as music director, the typical orchestra season consisted of three concerts. Occasional workshops, special events, and performances by small ensembles of orchestra members filled out the year. Some, but not all, members thought we could do more, and though the fourteen rehearsals that led up to each of those three concerts provided Oliver with time to work on basic ensemble problems, they also diluted the sense of urgency that the musicians felt as the concert approached. To quote Oliver:[7]

Concert weekends are intense. On concert weekends we rehearse on Thursday, Friday, and Saturday, with a warm-up/ mini-rehearsal on Sunday, the day of the concert. I am always amazed at the degree of commitment that the SFCO, as a whole, brings to performing, just in terms of time. Over the years, as the orchestra has improved, we have cut down the number of rehearsals per concert and added additional concerts. In 1999 there were three concerts; now there are five.

Sectional rehearsals, usually for string players, and also intense, have raised the level of quality. Prior to the first rehearsal in fall 2007 there were four string sectionals, more were scheduled, and two woodwind rehearsals were mixed in with full orchestra rehearsals. Important as orchestra ensemble is, concentrated work in homogeneous groups gets at the details that build overall quality.

New Works by New Mexico Composers

Over the years works by New Mexico composers have been sprinkled into formal concert programs. But the emphasis has changed in the past few years. To quote Oliver:[7]

> The Mill Atelier Foundation has been sponsoring our *New Works by New Mexico Composers* program, and we've had composers from Santa Fe, Los Lunas, Portales, Los Alamos, Albuquerque, Portales, Las Cruces and Grants participate. The composers have been high school students, amateurs, college students and faculty, established composers, and retired professionals. By and large we've managed to cover most all of the parts for every piece, even if it meant making twenty phone calls to fill out the trombone section, or hauling xylophones, marimbas, and other percussion equipment. What is most interesting is that we have always had an audience for the readings, and with minimal advertising. People in Santa Fe are interested in seeing what's new, and we've gotten very interesting submissions over the years. The fact that a standing orchestra at any level devotes three evenings a year to reading new works is remarkable, and, like all of our other programs, this one is free to the composers who participate.

> We have also presented, in the last four years, two concerts of works composed by members of the orchestra. We are lucky to have this kind of depth in the orchestra. Our composers include Jody Ellis, one of the founders of the orchestra; Bob Jones, an ASCAP composer; Ted Vives, an accomplished composer and arranger; John Michael Luther, who has had works performed by prominent musicians; and Gerry Fried, who has had a distinguished career in film, television,

and the concert hall. These concerts have been remarkable in their quality, their diversity, and amazingly, their coherence. We've always had an overture, a work with featured soloists, as well as works inspired and influenced by jazz, paintings, other cultures, or personal narrative.

Youth Concerts

Youth concerts and workshops, several noted earlier, encourage school-age children to become interested in music through concerts and educational programs. The orchestra now plays one or two hour-long programs for children in their Santa Fe elementary schools each year. We have learned that Oliver has a knack for involving children in those programs. We do the usual children's concerts routines—playing themes by individual instruments and putting various parts of the orchestra together to show how music is constructed—but soon the kids volunteer to be kings and queens, or Romeo and Juliet, or a panel of musical experts—and soon everyone is involved in the action, singing the themes, clapping out rhythms, and listening to music in a new way. Parents accompany their children, and at some events an interpreter provides a concurrent Spanish translation.

Oliver describes a poignant event at a youth concert: [7]

We performed a youth concert at the Santa Fe Indian School. At the time, we had a young Native American woman in the viola section, from Alaska, and she made me promise to let her say a few words at the concert. I had agreed, but with reluctance, as we only had an hour and I had no idea what she was planning to say or how long she would go on. But she convinced me, and kept referring to it as her "viola solo."

When I introduced her, she walked to the podium with a piece of paper in her hand, and the kids stopped talking, mostly. She said her name and what tribe she was from, and she read back her generations—I am the daughter of..., who was the son of... and she thanked the Indian School for inviting us to play a concert on their land. You could hear a pin drop, the silence was so profound. She talked about her musical ambitions and what playing in an orchestra meant to her. It was a great viola solo, and one of the most memorable experiences I've had in connection with the orchestra.

Anatomy of a Symphony Concert Previews

Several times each season, scheduled an hour prior to a Friday rehearsal, Oliver takes apart and puts back together some of the music scheduled for an upcoming concert. These programs provide insight into the lives of the composers, the construction of the music, and the rehearsal process. "Now let's hear that theme in the second trombone three bars after rehearsal letter C." "Now all the brass together at D." "Now that you've heard this theme you'll understand what I mean when I say 'Brahms was a lonely guy who didn't get out very much.'" These events have demonstrated the increasing confidence orchestra members and conductor have in each other. At first they were highly structured; dozens of extra rehearsal letters were penciled into parts. Now we just "wing it." The consummate lecturer, Oliver has the audience in rapt attention (and musicians in the orchestra learn more about the music they're playing, too).

Theme Concerts

Theme concerts include compositions selected around a

central concept. In the past few years themes have been American music, Scottish-inspired music, Spanish and Latin American music, music from Scandinavia, the world of opera, and works inspired by *Romeo and Juliet*. For example, the February 2001 Romeo and Juliet program included Tchaikovsky's *Romeo and Juliet Overture*, followed by excerpts from Berlioz's *Romeo and Juliet* and Prokofiev's *Romeo and Juliet*, interspersed with passages from Shakespeare's play, read by Theater Grottesco, a local theater company. The concert concluded with the *Symphonic Dances from West Side Story*. Theme concerts not only provide good material for publicity, but also one more way for audience members to learn about orchestral music.

Commissions

The orchestra's commissioning program has also been supported by the Mill Atelier Foundation. Commissioned works are rehearsed and performed at regular concerts along with the other works programmed. The commissioned works have been:

March 2003: Gerald Near, *A Festival Overture*. Gerald Near is a well known composer of works for organ, and choral works who was the director of music at Holy Faith Episcopal Church in Santa Fe.

June 2004: Christopher Berg, *We Have Heard the Chimes at Midnight*. The piece was inspired by the character *Falstaff* in Shakespeare's plays, as portrayed by Orson Welles in his cinematic syntheses based on the character.

June 2005: Panaiotis, *Northern Lights*. A part of the Northern Lights theme program, which featured composers from Scandinavia and Estonia. The piece was based on the phenomenon and the experience of the aurora borealis (northern lights) and scored for computer-generated sounds and orchestra.

April 2006: Gabriel Gonzales, *Allegro for Orchestra*. After his *Adagio* was played at one of the *New Works by New Mexico Composers* reading sessions, Gabriel Gonzales was invited to orchestrate a piece that he had previously written, a tongue-in-cheek pastiche based on music of the 18th and 19th centuries.

October 2007: Ron Strauss, *Time Flying*. A new piece by a Santa Fe composer.

A significant array of other new music, not formally commissioned, but performed by the orchestra in the last nine years, sets the course of the orchestra for innovation.

Other premieres by Santa Fe composers include *Prelude, Air and Capriccio for Alto Saxophone and Orchestra* by Robert C. Jones, *A Hamlet Overture* by Steven Paxton, and *Santa Fe, La Reyna* by Antonio Mendoza.

Writing about innovation and performance of orchestral music, Craig Smith, in a 2007 article, wrote: [12]

. . . In 23 years on Santa Fe's music scene, I've heard the same warhorses (or at least battle ponies) trotted out over and over by instrumental groups. Especially since the mid-1990s, safe repertoire and its repetition seem to be the order of the day. Am I experiencing apophenia—"the perception of connections and meaningfulness in unrelated things" as a medical dictionary puts it? I don't think so.

These days, the nonprofessional Santa Fe Community Orchestra presents more unusual repertoire—not necessarily ink-still-wet contemporary, but unfamiliar—than the Santa Fe Symphony Orchestra & Chorus, Santa Fe Pro Musica, the Santa Fe Concert Association in its year-end concerts, or even the New Mexico Symphony Orchestra. SFCO also gives modern music hearty support via regular reading sessions of New Mexico composers' works. (The other groups? Forget it.) The Santa Fe Desert Chorale, Canticum Novum, Pro Coro, Sangre de Cristo Chorale, and Santa Fe Women's Ensemble have a much higher ratio of unusual or contemporary music on their programs than our local orchestras. (The Santa Fe Opera is a case in itself, and deserves a whole column sometime.)

As Smith notes, professional groups have priorities relating to their bottom line that do not pertain in nearly the same strength to the community orchestra. The orchestra has had the luxury of time and commitment of its members to experiment with new music.

Administration

The Board of Directors is responsible for the administration of the orchestra. The board has grown along with the orchestra; development occurred in four overlapping phases.

- For the first twelve years the board operated in an informal manner. The president managed a bank account, dues were collected, and orchestra members and a few interested community members contributed funds to provide minimal remuneration for Bob Wingert and to meet other expenses. Peter Shoenfeld provided any needed legal advice.

- As budgets grew, the advantage of incorporating as a nonprofit organization became apparent. The Articles of Incorporation were approved March 18, 1994, with initial directors John Ward, David L. Brown, and Kathleen Clark. A revision of the bylaws was approved January 21, 2000, over the signature of then board president Laura Deanovic. Contributions began to be an important part of income. This second phase covers the period up to Oliver's appointment as music director for the 2000-01 season.

- During this second phase, the board acted essentially as a management committee, rather than just a governance and fundraising board. Members were elected casually, based on interest, enthusiasm, and commitment. The board, in its meetings, considered such details as concert dates, thank-you letters, expenses for individual music purchase/rental...Since there was no manager (except for one year, a 10-hour/week appointment), the details fell on the board. Thus Wingert and board presidents felt compelled to involve the board for approval of their decisions, and probably also to get the commitment necessary to take on the many detailed tasks required to support a growing orchestra, not the least of which was managing the grant process.

- With Oliver Prezant's appointment in 2000, the dynamics of relationships among music director, president, and the board changed. Oliver sought to clarify his responsibilities and authority, essentially to formalize the position of music director. Oliver provided leadership and urged the board to expand the orchestra's scope—more concerts, more grants, more management rigor, more support. Without that leadership, the orchestra would not have matured so rapidly, but the pressure on officers to keep up with the pace Oliver set took its toll. The culture of the board, whose members had been involved in all important decisions and wanted to continue that involvement, did not provide effective support. A few individuals stepped forward and took on important new tasks (e. g., support for new grants, organizing *Let's Dance!*).

- Beginning with the 2006-07 year, Paul Pease, newly elected president, took the board in a new direction. Board meetings occurred quarterly, the agenda contained policy issues and reports by officers, communication was by e-mail, and decisions were made by the president in consultation, where appropriate, with the executive committee or the full board. Information was distributed in advance, and board members were expected to be informed about issues and be familiar with data. It was a radical and necessary change.

- Two downsides of this transition will have to be accommodated: First, Paul has assumed responsibility for many of the details of managing the orchestra, including support for Oliver's new initiatives. That's a recipe for burnout. Second, those with experience on previous boards can be uncomfortable not being involved in such a wide range of decisions. The first issue would be ameliorated by funding a manager who reports to the president; the second by time and the successful growth of the organization.

The orchestra in 2007-08

Information and contact:

Visit the orchestra's website at www.sfco.org for information about scheduled concerts as well as general information about the orchestra. Send e-mail with questions or comments about the Santa Fe Community Orchestra to: music@sfco.org.

The orchestra's mailing address is:
Santa Fe Community Orchestra
551 W. Cordova Road, #211
Santa Fe, New Mexico 87505-1825
Telephone: (505) 466-4879

The Board of Directors and Officers for the 2007-08 year:

President	Paul Pease
Vice President:	James Preus
Treasurer	Anthony Grieco
Secretary	Lee Harvey
Member:	Richard Boyd
Member:	Michael Golden
Member:	Cissy de la Vallée
Member:	Mike Wagner
Member *ex officio*	Oliver Prezant

6

THE ELLIS PRIZE
FOR COMPOSITION

The Ellis Prize for Composition was established at the College of Santa Fe by Sunstone Press in 2008 in honor of Jody Ellis, a cello teacher and composer, and one of the founding members of the Santa Fe Community Orchestra in 1982, as well as the co-founder, along with Marcia Muth, of Sunstone Press in 1971. When asked about Sunstone's establishment of the Ellis Prize, which carries a cash award, Jim Smith, president of Sunstone, said, "Since Ms. Ellis has been such an inspiration to us at our publishing house and also such a force in the music community, we feel that by supporting the composition program in the music department at the College we will call attention to the outstanding talent that the College and the community has to offer."

Brendan Eder was the 2008 winner of the Ellis Prize. Eder is a composer, sound-engineer, and percussionist studying at the College of Santa Fe. He works as an engineer and producer in Los Angeles and Santa Fe and has had the honor of recording many remarkable musicians, one of them being Ray Pizzi. *Sinfonietta*, Eder's winning composition, is a brief exploration of different musical ideas. "I try to wrap my head around many ideas," he said. "It is a greater challenge than ever to create music guided by logic, principles, and dramatic reserve."

Mr. Eder's composition had its first reading by the Santa Fe Community Orchestra on March 14, 2008.

Left to right: Carl Condit of Sunstone Press and cellist in the Orchestra; Brendan Eder, winner of the 2008 Ellis Prize for Composition; and Jody Ellis, a cellist in the Orchestra and one of the founders.

7

IN CONCLUSION

Music, in one form or another, has been an integral part of the social and cultural life of Santa Fe for a century and a half. Distinguished soloists started to put Santa Fe on their itineraries in the 1930s. Orchestral music warmed up in the 1970s, with the Rio Grande Symphony and the first Santa Fe Symphony, and, in the 1980s, when the community orchestra was formed, it matured to its present configuration.

Arts activities contribute significantly to the Santa Fe economy[13] and while the community orchestra is not a financial contributor—not a major employer, not a magnet for tourist dollars—it has contributed to the overall cultural milieu for a quarter of a century. One audience survey showed that 12% of respondents were from outside New Mexico, and they learned about the concert from visits to the Museum of Fine Arts, adjacent to St. Francis Auditorium. Some of the current orchestra members chose to retire here in part because the orchestra presented an opportunity to perform with a symphony orchestra.

While an important purpose of the orchestra is to provide an outlet for amateur (and some professional) musicians to rehearse and perform together, the mission statement and programs of the Santa Fe Community Orchestra address several other objectives—stimulate compositions by local composers, provide a venue for talented young musicians, engage young people in youth activities and concerts, introduce people to orchestra music so they will support professional organizations, et cetera—but they can be pursued only if the members of the orchestra are engaged, committed, disciplined, supportive, and enthusiastic.

They will be so if there is good leadership, stimulating music, and expectations that fit the characteristics of members. This review of the orchestra's first two decades shows that, whether by design or good luck, that has been the case. We have been led to more music and a higher level of musicianship, sometimes dragging our feet at the increased commitment it places on us. Nevertheless, the orchestra has come a long way, particularly over the past nine years of Oliver Prezant's leadership.

I hope that when some member writes a 50-year history s/he will describe the continued development of the program and competence of the orchestra and the contributions of those, noted here, who came before.

NOTES

1. Jean R. Padilla, "Santa Fe's Own Music Men and Women: Los Conquistadores Band" (unpublished paper, January 1992). (See www.santafeconcertband.org for a full copy of this paper)
2. Anne-Lise Cohen, "Santa Fe Community Orchestra: A Short History" (unpublished paper, 1983).
3. William Dunning, "Three Orchestras for Santa Fe" The Santa Fe New Mexican, November 1983.
4. Craig Smith, review, The Santa Fe New Mexican, November 4, 1990.
5. Craig Smith, "Grinage, Orchestra share mutual musical enthusiasm," The Santa Fe New Mexican, December 1, 1989.
6. Craig Smith, "New Directions for the Community Orchestra," The Santa Fe New Mexican, October 8, 1999, Pasatiempo, p. 54.
7. Oliver Prezant, personal communication, 2007.
8. Fauntleroy, Gussie, The Santa Fe New Mexican, May 9, 1999, p. E6.
9. Bernie Van der Hoeven, "Survey of Occupations" (unpublished paper, 2003).
10. Kay Lockridge, The Santa Fe New Mexican, November 13, 2005, p. E3.
11. Pat Greathouse, "The Turkey Lady's Long Journey Home," The Santa Fe New Mexican, December 14, 2005.
12. Craig Smith, The Santa Fe New Mexican, February 23, 2007.
13. Jeffrey Mitchell and Lee A. Reynis, "The Economic Importance of the Arts and Cultural Industries in Santa Fe County" (research report, UNM Bureau of Business and Economic Research, November 2004).
14. Five of the photographs in this book are © 2007 by InsightFoto.com and are reproduced by permission.

The author conducted telephone conversations with Bob Wingert and Martha Dean Kerr in June of 2007. The author also interviewed a group of people together who were members in 1982: Jody Ellis, Mary Ann Martinez, Willard Chilcott, Donald Vasquez, and Peter Shoenfeld. Additionally, he interviewed Anne-Lise Cohen, Jody Ellis, Harold Geller, Pat Greathouse, Greg Heltman, Mary Ann Martinez, Wendy McGuire, Paul Pease, Oliver Prezant, Bernard Rubenstein, and Lisa Van Sickle.

APPENDIX I

Santa Fe Community Orchestra
Concert Programs and Soloists

Information about music and soloists was taken from concert programs and may not reflect last-minute changes.

Concert on 7/5/1982

Beethoven / *Turkish March from "The Ruins of Athens" Op. 113, No. 4*
Brahms / *Hungarian Dance No. 5*
Haydn / *Symphony No. 104 in D Major ("London")*
Liadov / *Eight Russian Folk Songs, Op. 58*
Strauss, J. / *The Emperor Waltz*

Concert on 11/19/1982

Barber / *Adagio for Strings*
Juan Crisostomo Arriaga y Balzola / *Overture to "Los esclavos felices"*
Sibelius / *Symphony No. 2 in D, Op. 43*

Concert on 3/13/1983

Beethoven / *Short Pieces for Wind Ensemble*
de Falla / *The Three-Cornered Hat*
Grieg / *Piano Concerto in A Minor,* June De Toth, pianist
Schubert / *Symphony No. 6 in C Major*

Concert on 6/12/1983

Agay / *Five Easy Dances,* Aeolian Wind Quintet
Bergsma / *Paul Bunyan Suite*
Borodin / *On the Steppes of Central Asia*
Copland / *An Outdoor Overture (1938)*

Frescobaldi (Hans-Kindler) / *Toccata*
Purcell (Perry) / *Trumpet Tune & Air*
Rimsky-Korsakov / *Capriccio Espagnol, Op. 34*

Concert on 8/2/1983

Arriaga / *Overture to "Los Esclavos Felices"*
Chabrier / *España/Spanish Rhapsody*
de Falla / *Three Dances from "El Sombrero de Tres Picos"*
Smetana / *Three Dances from "The Bartered Bride"*
Vaughan Williams (Greaves) / *Fantasia on "Greensleeves"*

Concert on 11/12/1983

Brahms / *Variations on a Theme by Haydn, Op. 36*
Glinka / *"Ruslan & Lyudmila" Overture*
Haydn / *Cello Concerto in C,* Laurel Rogers, cellist
Rimsky-Korsakov / *Capriccio Espagnol, Op. 34*

Concert on 4/8/1984

Berlioz / "Roman Carnival" Overture, Opus 9
Fauré / *Pavane*
Mahler / Lieder eines fahrenden Gesellen / (Songs of a Wayfarer),
Rosemarie Caminiti, soprano
Mozart / Overture to "The Abduction from the Seraglio,"
K. 384
Stravinsky / *Suite pour Petit Orchestra (No. 1)*

Concert on 7/3/1984

Bernstein / *Overture to "Candide"*
Copland / *Selections from "Rodeo"*
Fauré (Snider) / *Pavane*
Haydn / *"Toy" Symphony*
Sousa / *Stars & Stripes Forever*
Strauss, J / *Tales from the Vienna Woods*
Strauss, J. / *Polka "Unter Donner und Blitz"*

Concert on 11/18/1984

Beethoven / *Symphony No. 7 in A Major*
Lawrence / *The "Sneetches,"* Robert Saam, narrator
Rossini / *Overture to "La Gazza Ladra"*

Concert on 3/24/1985

Bach (Ormandy) / *Chorale Prelude "Wachet auf, ruft uns die Stimme"*
Bach (Stokowski) / *"Komm Susser Tod"*
Bartók / *Rumanian Folk Dances*
Felix Mendelssohn / *Concerto in E Minor, Op. 64, for Violin & Orchestra,* Lynn D. Case, violinist
Haydn (Hans Gal) / *Overture to "Armida"*

Concert on 7/3/1985.

Bernstein / *Suite from "West Side Story"*
Bizet / *Selections from "Carmen"*
de Falla / *Spanish Dance No. 1 from "La Vida Breve"*
Gershwin / *Cuban Overture*
Romero / *Four Pieces for Guitar & Orchestra,* Ruben Romero, guitarist
Vivaldi / *Concerto in A Minor,* Suzuki Children String Ensemble
Vivaldi / *Concerto for Guitar,* Ruben Romero, guitarist

Concert on 11/24/1985

Bach (Anton Webern) / *Fugue for Six Voices from "The Musical Offering"*
Debussy (M. Ravel) / *Sarabande and Danse*
Handel / *Overture "Theodora"*
Mozart / *Concerto for Flute & Harp in C Major, K. 299,* Rosalind Simpson, harpist; Shelby Boggio, flutist

Concert on 3/23/1986

Beethoven / *Symphony No. 6 in F Major, Op. 68, "Pastoral"*
Copland / *Music from "The Red Pony"*

Marcello / *Concerto in C Minor for Oboe and Strings*, Elaine M. Grossman, oboist

Concert on 7/6/1986

Anonymous / *Sonata*
Bach-Stokowski / *"Komm Susser Tod"*
Beethoven / *Overture to "Egmont"*
Chrisiansen, Richard / *"Te Deum" for Organ & Orchestra*, Richard Christiansen, organist
Handel / *Music for the Royal Fireworks*
Susato, Tillman / *Three Dances*

Concert on 11/15/1986

McLaughlin, Jennifer / *Out for Clarinet & Orchestra*, Robert Wingert, clarinetist
Schubert / *Incidental Music from "Rosamunde"*
Shostakovich / *Festival Overture*
Wagner (Baermann) / *Adagio for Clarinet & Strings*, Robert Wingert, clarinetist

Concert on 4/5/1987

Bach / *Magnificat*, Santa Fe Community College Chorus
Mendelssohn / *Overture to "Ruy Blas"*
Salmenhaara, Erkki / *Adagietto*
Sibelius / *Incidental Music to "King Christian II"*

Concert on 6/13/1987

Berlioz / *"Roman Carnival" Overture*
Fauré / *Pavane*
Rossini / *Overture to "La Gazza Ladra"*
Smetana / *Three Dances from "The Bartered Bride"*
Strauss, J. / *"Emperor Waltz"*

Concert on 11/15/1987

Mauldin, Michael / *Promontory Night*
Tchaikovsky / *Symphony No. 5 in E Minor, Op. 64*
Telemann / *Suite in F Major for Two Horns, Strings, & Continuo*,
Joel and Beth Scott, horns

Concert on 3/20/1988

de Falla / *Miller's Dance*, William Hinrichs, narrator
Schubert / *Unfinished Symphony*, Charles Bell, narrator
Shostakovich / *Symphony No. 1 (First Movement)*, Vladimir
Gerhanouk, narrator,
Toyama, Yuzo / *Divertimento*, Yuiko Tsutoma, narrator
Vaughn Williams / *English Folk Song Suite*, Lillian Taylor, narrator

Concert on 6/12/1988

Moussorgsky / *Night on Bald Mountain*
Mozart / *Divertimento No. 3 in E-flat Major, K. 166*
Purcell / *Music to "Midsummer Night's Dream"*
Strauss, J. / *Waltz "Wo di Citronen Blueh'n," Op. 364*

Concert on 11/27/1988

Forman, Joanne / *Vida, Overture to a Modern Novel*
Grieg / *Suite for Strings in Olden Style (from Holberg's time), Op. 40*
Stravinsky / *Symphonies of Wind Instruments*
Stravinsky / *Circus Polka*
Wagner / *Prelude to "Die Meistersinger"*

Concert on 4/9/1989

Bizet / *Duo from "Carmen,"* Sandra Dudek-Twibell, mezzo-soprano;
Doug Blakely, tenor
Bizet / *Entre'act from "Carmen"*
Humperdinck / *Prayer and Dream Sequence from "Hansel and Gretel,"* Gail Springer, soprano
Mascagni / *Intermezzo from "Cavalleria Rusticana"*

Mascagni / *"Voi lo sapete" from "Cavalleria Rusticana,"* Sandra Dudek-Twibell, mezzo-soprano

Menotti / *"I shall find for you..." from "The Counsel,"* Gail Springer, soprano

Mozart / *Overture to "The Magic Flute"*

Rossini / *"Non piu mesta" from "Cinderella,"* Sandra Dudek-Twibell, mezzo-soprano

Sondheim / *"Green Finch and Linnet Bird" from "Sweeney Todd,"* Gail Springer, soprano

Strauss, J. / *Trio from "Die Fledermaus,"* Gail Springer, soprano; Sandra Dudek Twibell, mezzo-soprano; Doug Blakely, tenor

Verdi / *"Ma se m'e forze perderti" from "Masked Ball,"* Doug Blakely, tenor

Verdi / *Prelude to Act III, "La Traviata"*

Concert on 11/19/1989

Arriaga, Juan / *Overture to "Los Esclavos Felices"*

Chopin / *Piano Concerto No. 1 in E Minor,* Ronald Grinage, pianist

Schubert / *Music from "Rosamunde"*

Concert on 4/8/1990

Beethoven / *Symphony No. 5 in C Minor*

McLaughlin / *The Distance of the Moon*

Mozart / *Concerto for Horn & Orchestra, No 3 in E Major, K. 447,* John Petring, horn

Concert on 6/24/1990

Fauré / *Elegie for Solo Cello, Op. 24,* Rebecca Caron, cellist

Sibelius / *The Swan of Tuonela, Op. 22,* Dennis Calvin, English horn

Liadov / *Eight Russian Folk Songs, Op. 58*

Mozart / *Overture to "The Abduction from the Seraglio," K. 38*

Mozart / *Two Entr'actes from "Thamos, King of Egypt"*

Riegger / *Dance Rhythms, Op. 58*

Concert on 11/4/1990

Castelnuovo-Tedesco / *Concerto for Harp and Orchestra,* Rosalind Simpson, harpist
Handel / *Overture to "Judas Maccabeus"*
Jacob / *Suite in F for Small Orchestra*
Smetana / *"The Moldau" from "Ma Vlast"*

Concert on 4/7/1991

Mozart / *Symphony No. 27 in G Major, K. 199*
Mozart / *Concertone in C Major for Two Violins and Orchestra, K. 190,* Tom & Charmaine Weber, violinists
Mozart / *Gran Partita for Wind Instruments, No. 10 in B-flat Major, K. 361*

Concert on 6/16/1991

Bach / *Sinfonia*
Bartók / *Music for Children*
Berlioz / *Hungarian March, Op. 24*
Dvorak / *Slavonic Dances, Op. 46*
Jakubenas, Vladas / *Rapsodija*
Janacek / *Lachian Dances, Op. 2*

Concert on 11/24/1991

Handel / *Concerto for Organ & Orchestra, Op. 4, No. 5,* Rebecca Rollett, organist
Mozart / *Symphony No. 40 in G, K. 550*
Mozart / *German Dances, K. 509*

Concert on 4/5/1992

Beethoven / *"Coriolan" Overture, Op. 62*
Beethoven / *Symphony No. 1 in C, Op. 21*
Brahms / *"Nanie," Op. 178,* Santa Fe Community Chorus
Mozart / *"Ave Verum Corpus," K. 618,* Santa Fe Community Chorus

Concert on 6/21/1992

de Hartmann, Thomas / *Concierto Andaluz, Op. 81*, Marylinda Gutierrez, flutist
Bizet / *Intermezzo from "Carmen,"* Lili del Castillo, dancer
Bizet / *"Les Toreadors" from "Carmen,"* Lili del Castillo, dancer
Bizet / *"Seguedilla" from "Carmen,"* Lili del Castillo, dancer
Bizet / *"Aragonaise" from "Carmen,"* Lili del Castillo, dancer
Capuzzi, Giuseppe / *Concerto for Violone,* John Clark, double bass
Granados / *"Intermezzo" from Goyescas*
Rodrigo / *Tres Viejo Aires de Danze*
Turina / *Oración del Torero, Op. 34*

Concert on 11/22/1992

Beethoven / *Symphony No. 7 in A, Op. 92*
Ditters von Dittersdorf, Karl / *Concerto for Harp & Orchestra,* Rosalind Simpson, harpist
McLaughlin / *The Distance of the Moon*

Concert on 3/30/1993

Berg, Christopher / *"A Lover's Cosmology & the Meaning of Hell,"* Janice Felty, mezzo-soprano
Berg, Christopher / *"From Not Waving but Drowning,"* Janice Felty, mezzo-soprano
Franck (orch Busser) / *Four excerpts from "The Organist"*
Poulenc / *Two Marches and an Interlude*
Schoenberg (orch Wingert) / *Canon*

Concert on 4/4/1993

Bartók / *Rumanian Folk Dances*
Berg, Christopher / *"From Not Waving but Drowning,"* Janice Felty. mezzo-soprano
Haydn / *Symphony No. 101 in D ("The Clock")*
Schubert / *Overture to "Die Zwillingsbruder"*

Concert on 6/13/1993

Grieg / *Piano Concerto in A, Op. 92*, June De Toth, pianist
Shoenfeld, Nina / *Light Suite for Orchestra*
Wagner / *Overture to "Rienzi"*

Concert on 12/5/1993

Brahms / *Symphony No. 1 in C, Op. 68*
Puccini / *Aria from "Turandot," Act 1*, Sandra Twibell, soprano
Puccini / *"Vissi d'arte, vissi d'amore," from "Tosca"*, Sandra Twibell, soprano
von Weber / *"Ozean, Du Ungeheuer" Aria from "Oberon,"* Sandra Twibell, soprano
von Weber / *Overture to "Oberon"*

Concert on 3/27/1994

Bach / *Brandenburg Concerto No. 3 in G, BWV 1048*, Martha Dean Kerr, violin; Tom Terwilliger, cello; Kathleen McIntosh, harpsichord
Respighi / *Gli Uccelli (The Birds)*
Strauss, R / *Serenade for Winds in E-flat, Op. 7*
Valjean, Paul / *Three Lyrics for Oboe, Bassoon & Strings*, Richard Hall, bassoon; Elaine Heltmann, oboe
Vivaldi / *Concerto in E for Bassoon & Strings*, Richard Hall, bassoon

Concert on 6/12/1994

Dvorak / *Legends, Op. 59, Nos. 1-3*
Dvorak / *Romance in F for Violin & Orchestra, Op. 11*, Justin Pollak, violinist
Fibich, Zdenek / *A Night at Karlstein, Comedy Overture*
Janacek / *Adagio for Orchestra*
Janacek / *Lachian Dance, No. 1*
Mozart / *Overture to "La Clemenza di Tito," K. 621*
Napravnik, Eduard / *Romance from Two Spanish Pieces*

Concert on 11/20/1994

Beethoven / *"The Creatures of Prometheus"*
Krommer / *Concerto for Two Clarinets & Orchestra,* Eddie Daniels
& Robert Wingert, clarinetists
Marti, Heinz / *Passacaglia for Orchestra*

Concert on 4/2/1995

Borodin / *Symphony No. 2 in B Major*
Ellis / *Too Late*
Haydn / *Concerto for Cello & Orchestra in C Major,* Ruth
Sommers, cellist

Concert on 6/11/1995

Brahms / *Serenade No. 1 in D, Op. 11*
Hindemith / *Introductory Piece for Orchestra*
Mozart / *Sinfonia Concertante in E-flat,* Lynn Ledbetter, violin;
Robert Radner, viola

Concert on 11/17/1995

Barber / *"Knoxville: Summer of 1915,"* Theresa Coggeshall, soprano
Brahms / *Academic Festival Overture*
Copland / *Fanfare for the Common Man*
Granados / *Enrique Goyescas: Intermezzo*
Prokofiev / *Romeo and Juliet: Suite No. 2, Op. 64*

Concert on 6/6/1996

Grieg / *Peer Gynt Suite No. 1*
Kraus, Joseph Martin / *Sinfonie in C Minor*
Suolahti, Heikki / *Sinfonia Piccola*

Concert on 12/8/1996

Chopin / *Piano Concerto No. 2,* Maya Hoffman
Mozart / *Overture to "Don Giovanni"*

Paulus, Stephen / *Manhattan Sinfonietta*
Schumann, Robert / *Scenes from the East, Op. 66*

Concert on 4/20/1997

Collins / *Spring Flowers,* James Pellerite, native flute
Dvorak / *Symphony No. 8 in C Minor*
Marcello, Alessandro / *Concerto in C Minor, adapted for Native Flute & Orchestra,* James Pellerite
Muczynski, Robert / *Dovetail Overture*

Concert on 6/8/1997

Arriaga, Juan C. / *Overture to "Los Esclavos Felices"*
de Falla, Manuel / *El Amor Brujo: Ballet Suite*
Rodrigo, Joaquin / *Concierto de Aranjuez,* Anna Maria Padilla, guitarist
Turina, Joaquin / *La Oración del Torero*

Concert on 11/23/1997

Bruch, Max / *"Kol Nidrei" for Cello and Orchestra,* Laurel Rogers, cellist
Copland / *Music from "The Red Pony"*
Ellis, Jody / *A Circle of Seasons*
Gershwin / *Cuban Overture*
Handel / *Concerto for Harp in B-flat Major,* Rosalind Simpson, harpist
Saint-Saens / *"The Swan" from "Carnival of the Animals,"* Laurel Rogers, cellist

Concert on 4/5/1998

Beethoven / *Symphony No. 7 in A Major, Op. 92*
Humperdinck / *Prelude to "Hansel and Gretel"*
Mozart / *Piano Concerto No. 24 in C Minor,* Maya Hoffman, pianist

Concert on 6/14/1998

Beethoven / *Sextet for Two Horns and Strings*, Beth and Joel Scott, horns
Berlioz, Hector / *"Roman Carnival" Overture*
Gounod, Charles / *Petite Symphonie for Winds*
Muczynski, Robert / *Charade*
Vivaldi, Antonio / *Concerto in G Minor for Two Cellos, RV 331*, Richard Hall & James Preus, bassoonists

Concert on 11/22/1998

Oliver Prezant, Guest Conductor

Beethoven / *Symphony No. 1 in C Major, Op. 21*
Jacob, Gordon / *Old Wine in New Bottles*
Mozart / *Divertimento in F Major, K. 138*
Sarasate, Pablo de / *Zigeunerweisen*, Elena Sopoci, violinist
Vaughn Williams, Ralph / *"The Lark Ascending,"* Elena Sopoci, violinist

Concert on 3/28/1999

Beethoven / *Egmont Overture, Op. 84*
Cowell, Henry / *Hymn and Fuguing Tune No. 2*
Hummel, Johann Nepomuk / *Concerto for Trumpet and Orchestra*, Greg Heltman, trumpet
Felix Mendelssohn / *Symphony No. 3, Op. 56, "Scottish"*

Concert on 6/13/1999

Bloch, Ernest / *Suite Hebraique for Viola and Orchestra*, Britt Ravnan, violist
Copland, Aaron / *Selections from "Rodeo"*
Mendelssohn, Felix / *Overture: The Hebrides ("Fingal's Cave"), Op. 26*
Schumann, Robert / *Konzert fur Violoncello, Op. 129*, Tom Terwilliger, cellist
Tchaikovsky / *Overture: Romeo and Juliet*

Concert on 10/10/1999

Andriessen, Hendrik / *Variations on a Theme by Couperin, for Flute, Harp, and Strings,* Mary Ann Martinez, flutist; Rosalind Simpson, harpist
Brahms / *Symphony No. 2 in D Major, Op. 73*
Hindemith, Paul / *Orchestral Suite: Nobilissima Visione*

Concert on 11/21/1999

Beethoven / *Symphony No. 6 in F Major, "Pastoral," Op. 68*
Copland, Aaron / *Fanfare for the Common Man,* Santa Fe Brass Quintet
Gabrieli, Giovanni / *Canzon Duodecini Toni for Ten Part Brass Choir*
P.D.Q. Bach / *Fanfare for the Common Cold*
Rautavaara, Einojuhani / *Cantus Articus: Concerto for Birds and Orchestra, Op. 61*
Tower, Joan / *Fanfare for the Uncommon Woman, No. 2,* Santa Fe Brass Quintet

Concert on 4/16/2000

Chavez, Carlos / *Sinfonie India (Symphony No. 2)*
Dvorak / *Symphony No. 9 in E Minor, Op. 95, "From the New World"*
Gershwin / *Rhapsody in Blue,* Kelvin McNeal, pianist

Concert on 6/11/2000

Bach / *"Vivace" from Concerto in D Minor for Two Violins and Strings,* Suzuki violin students
Catalani, Alfredo / *"Ebben? Ne andro lontana" from "La Wally,"* Mary Ann Fellows, soprano
Mozart / *Overture from "Così fan tutte"*
Mozart / *"Come scoglio immote resta,"* Mary Ann Fellows, soprano
Strauss, Johann / *"Czardas" from "Die Fledermaus,"* Mary Ann Fellows, soprano
Tchaikovsky / *Symphony No. 1, Op. 13*

Vivaldi / *Concerto for Flute and String Orchestra,* Mary Ann Martinez, flutist

Concert on 10/15/2000

Dukas, Paul / *Fanfare from "La Peri"*
Jones, Robert C. / *Prelude, Air and Capriccio for Alto Saxophone and Chamber Orchestra,* Robert C. Jones
Kodaly, Zoltan / *Dances from Galanta*
Mozart / *Serenade in C Minor, K. 388*
Schumann, Robert / *Symphony No. 3 in E-flat Major, Op. 97, "Rhenish"*

Concert on 12/3/2000

Bach / *Orchestral Suite No. 3 in D Major, BWV 1068*
Saint-Saens, Camille / *Symphony No. 3 in C Minor, Op. 78,* Linda Raney, organist
Torke, Michael / *December*

Concert on 2/11/2001

Berlioz, Hector / *Romeo and Juliet, from Op. 17,* Theater Grottesco
Bernstein, Leonard / *Symphonic Dances from "West Side Story"*
Prokofiev, Sergei / *Romeo and Juliet, 2nd Suite*
Tchaikovsky / *Romeo and Juliet, Fantasy Overture*

Concert on 4/22/2001

Holst, Gustav / *"The Planets," Op. 32*
Mahler, Gustav / *Symphony No. 4, 1st Movement*
Sibelius, Jean / *Violin Concerto in C Minor, Op. 47,* Veronique Marcel, violinist

Concert on 6/10/2001

Barber, Samuel / *Overture to the "School for Scandal"*
Elgar, Sir Edward / *Variations on an Original Theme, Op. 36, "Enigma"*

Saint-Saens, Camille / *Cello Concerto No. 1 in A Minor, Op. 33,* James Knudson, cellist

Concert on 10/21/2001

Dvorak, Antonin / *Largo from Symphony No. 9, "From the New World"*
Handel / *Concerto Grosso in C*
Sibelius, Jean / *Symphony No. 2 in D Major*
Ward/Bates / *America the Beautiful*

Concert on 12/9/2001

Barber, Samuel / *"Knoxville: Summer of 1915," Op. 24,* Theresa Coggeshall, soprano
Bartók, Bela / *Tanz-Suite (Movements I through III)*
Bernstein, Leonard / *Overture to "Candide"*
Brahms / *Symphony No. 3 in F Major, Op. 90*

Concert on 3/10/2002

Beethoven / *Symphony No. 9,* Louise Mendius, Tim Willson, Consuelo Sanudo, Loren Jacobson

Concert on 4/21/2002

Hovhaness, Alan / *Prayer of St. Gregory,* Michael Ebinger, trumpet
Moussorgsky, Modest / *Pictures at an Exhibition*
Respighi, Ottorino / *Ancient Dances and Airs (Suite)*
Rimsky-Korsakov / *Concerto for Trombone (arr Vives),* Ted Vives, trombonist

Concert on 6/9/2002

Albeniz, Isaac / *Evocation de La Suite "Iberia"*
Ginastera, Alberto / *Concerto for Harp and Orchestra,* Rosalind Simpson, harpist
Jimez/Burgas / *Las Bodas de Luis Alonso (arr Ted Vives),* Mariachi El Tigre

Mendoza, Antonio / *Santa Fe La Reyna*
Mendoza, Antonio / *Violin Huapango (arr Ted Vives)*, Pablo Huspango
Ramirez, Elpido / *La Malaquelia (arr Robert C. Jones)*, Mariachi El Tigre
Ravel, Maurice / *Rapsodie Espagnole*

Concert on 10/27/2002

Dvorak / *Symphony No. 8, Op. 88*
Mozart / *Sinifonia Concertante*, Gerald Fried, oboist; Michael Golden, clarinetist; Elizabeth Hunke, horn; James Preus, bassonist
Wagner / *Prelude to "Die Meistersinger"*

Concert on 12/15/2002

Strauss, Jr. / *Overture from "Die Fledermaus," Op. 362*
Tchaikovsky / *Symphony No. 5 in E Minor, Op. 64*
Vanhal, Johann Baptist / *Concerto for Double Bass*, John Ebinger, bassist

Concert on 2/2/2003

Ellis, Jody / *The Ancient Ones (Anazazi)*
Fried, Gerald / *Time Travel for Oboe and Orchestra*
Jones, Robert C. / *Four Symphonic Images*
Vives, Ted / *Introduction and Overture*

Concert on 3/9/2003

Borodin, Alexander / *In the Steppes of Central Asia*
Britten, Benjamin / *Young Person's Guide to the Orchestra, Op. 34*
Near, Gerald / *Premiere: A Festive Overture*
Rachmaninoff / *Piano Concerto No. 2, Op. 18*, Kelvin McNeal, pianist

Concert on 4/24/2003

Brahms / *Symphony No. 1, Op. 68*
Debussy, Claude / *La Mer*

Mozart / *Overture to "Magic Flute," K. 620*

Concert on 6/3/2003

Fibitch, Zdenek / *Selanka (Pastorale),* Robert Wingert, clarinetist
Maxwell Davies, Sir Robert / *An Orkney Wedding, With Sunrise,* Don Machen, bagpiper
Mendelssohn, Felix / *Symphony No. 3, "Scottish"*
von Weber, Carl Maria / *Concertino for Clarinet, Op. 26,* Robert Wingert, clarinetist

Concert on 10/19/2003

Beethoven / *Symphony No. 5, Op. 67*
Mahler, Gustav / *Songs of a Wayfarer,* Susannah Tyrell, soprano
Mendelssohn, Felix / *Overture: "A Midsummer Night's Dream"*

Concert on 12/7/2003

Debussy, Claude / *Premiere Rhapsodie for Clarinet and Orchestra,* James Preus, clarinetist
Paxton, Steven / *A Hamlet Overture*
Prokofiev, Sergei / *Symphony No. 5 in B-flat Major, Op. 100*
Vivaldi, Antonio / *Concerto in A Minor for Bassoon and Strings, F, VIII No.7,* Debra Poulin, bassoonist

Concert on 1/16/2004

Cooper, James Medary / *Dream Sketches, Suite for Orchestra*
Jones, Robert C. / *Chaconne a son Gout*

Concert on 2/27/2004

Badarak, Mary Lynn Place / *Amanecer, for Chamber Orchestra*
Dal Porto, Mark / *Life's Vanity, for Soprano and Orchestra*
Paxton, Steven / *Three Doors, for Symphony Orchestra*

Concert on 3/7/2004

Orff, Carl / *"Carmina Burana,"* Joanna Morska-Osinska, Kent Wall, Brian Podolny

Concert on 3/19/2004

Egenes, John / *Virginia Home, for Strings*
Schneider, Gregory Alan / *Melancholy Prelude, for String Orchestra*

Concert on 4/25/2004

Mendelssohn, Felix / *Violin Concerto in E Minor, Op. 64*, Martha Caplin, violinist
Rossini, Gioachino / *Overture to "La Gazza Ladra"*
Sibelius, Jean / *Symphony No. 5, Op. 82*

Concert on 6/6/2004

Adams, John / *Short Ride in a Fast Machine*
Barber, Samuel / *Overture to the "School for Scandal"*
Berg, Christopher / *We Have Heard the Chimes at Midnight*
Copland, Aaron / *Appalachian Spring*
Ives, Charles / *Symphony No. 3: "The Camp Meeting"*

Concert on 10/17/2004

Dukas, Paul / *Fanfare from "La Peri"*
Gershwin, arr Jones / *A Gershwin Sampler,* Ron Grinage, pianist
Mozart / *Symphony 39 in E-flat Major, K. 543*
Shostakovich, Dimitri / *Concerto No. 2 for Piano and Orchestra, Op. 102*, Ron Grinage, pianist
Stravinsky Igor / *Symphonies of Winds*

Concert on 12/5/2004

Brahms / *Academic Festival Overture, Op. 80*
Brahms / *Alto Rhapsodie, Op. 53*, Jacqueline Zander-Wall, alto;
Santa Fe Men's Camerata

Brahms / *Symphony No. 4 in E Minor, Op. 98*

Concert on 4/17/2005

Marquez, Arturo / *Danzon No. 2*
Milhaud, Darius / Concerto *for Percussion & Chamber Orchestra,*
Stuart Bloom, timpanist
Mozart / *Concerto No. 3 for Horn in E-flat, K. 447,* Steven Ovitsky,
horn
Saint-Saens, Camille / *Symphony No. 3, Op. 78, "Organ Symphony,"*
Frederick Fox, organist

Concert on 6/5/2005

Grieg, Edvard / *Peer Gynt Suite No. 1, Op. 46*
Nielsen, Carl / *Helios Overture*
Panaiotis / *Northern Lights*
Pärt, Arvo / *Fratres (Brothers),* Britt Ravnan, violinist
Sibelius, Jean / *Symphony No. 7, Op. 105*

Concert on 10/16/2005

Berlioz, Hector / *Symphonie Fantastique, Op. 14*
Bernstein, Leonard / *Overture to "Candide"*
Castelnuovo-Tedesco, M. / *Concerto for Guitar and Orchestra, Op.
99,* Brian DeLay, guitarist

Concert on 12/4/2005

Humperdinck, Englelbert / *Prelude to "Hansel and Gretel"*
Smetana, Bedrich / *The Moldau (Vltava)*
Stravinsky, Igor / *Suite: "The Firebird"*
Wagner, Richard / *Prelude and Isolde's Love Death from "Tristan and
Isolde"*

Concert on 3/5/2006

Verdi, Giuseppe / *Requiem,* Marilyn Barnes, Monika Cosson-Sheppard,
Andre Garcia-Nuthmann, Frederick Fox

Concert on 4/23/2006

Debussy, Claude / *Prelude to "The Afternoon of a Faun"*
Dvorak, Antonin / *Concerto for Cello and Orchestra, second movement*, Dina Sassone, cellist
Tchaikovsky / *Francesca da Rimini*

Concert on 6/4/2006

Cimarosa, Domenico / *Concerto for Oboe and Strings*, Gerald Fried, oboist
Gonzales, Gabriel / *Allegro for Orchestra*
Mahler, Gustav / *Symphony No. 4*

Concert on 10/15/2006

Hovhaness, Alan / *"Mysterious Mountain" (Symphony No. 2), Op. 132*
Mozart / *Symphony No. 29 in A Major, K. 201*
Strauss, Richard / *Tod und Verklarung (Death and Transfiguration), Op 24*

Concert on 12/3/2006

Mariachi Selections, Mariachi Juvenil
Franck, César / *Symphony in D Minor*
Prokofiev / *Violin Concerto No. 2 in G Minor, Op. 3*, Margaret Carpenter, violinist

Concert on 3/4/2007

Ellis, Jody / *The Dreams of Kokopelli*
Fried, Gerald / *The "Roots" Suite*
Jones, Robert / *Orchestra Variations on "L 'Homme Armee"*
Vives, Ted / *Children's Suite*

Concert on 4/15/2007

Brahms / *Symphony No. 3 in F*
Hummel, Johann Nepomuk / *Trumpet Concerto in E Major*, Amanda

Pepping, trumpet
Rossini / *Overture to "The Italian Girl in Algiers"*

Concert on 5/3/2007

Bizet / *"Carmen" (Highlights)*
Massenet, Offenbach, Puccini, Rossini, & Verdi / *Arias*, Monika
Cosson-Sheppard, Jacqueline Zander-Wall, Roberto Gomez, Kevin
Calloway

APPENDIX II

Musicians Who Have Played in the
Santa Fe Community Orchestra

Information from Concert Programs
(Numbers following names indicate number of concerts
played 1982-2007)

BASS

Josh Allen-Flowers 3
Janet Bajan 8
Robert Bell 23
Miriam Blake 18
Raymond Blanchett 1
John Clark 8
Greg Clemmons 1
Julius Cahn 3
Dale Covington 1
Michael Dillon 1
John Ebinger 2
Jeanne Fair 11
Stephen Goldman 8
JoAnne Key Harrington 1
Ronda Kay 1
James Maldonado 1
Jim Martinez 4
Joe Mondragon 3
John Montoya 1
John O'Dell 2
Ross Palmer 30
Emily Petty 5
Lexi Powell 1
Terry Pruitt 1
Peter Shoenfeld 75

Richard Snider 18
Lenny Tischler 25
Ryan Walker 1
Pat Whitney 3
Nat Wilson 4

BASS CLARINET

Richard Baldinger 36
Tom Brooks 2
Barbara Cohn 2
Manuel Mandel 6
Dean Perry 1
Richard Snider 18

BASSOON

Patrick Berry 25
Cal Deater 25
Judy Deater 23
Artemus Edwards 1
Richard Hall 8
Karl Johnson 6
Robert Kelly 2
Richard Lehnart 1

Scott Oakes 4
Debra Poulin 11
James Preus 48
Paula Robinson 1
Adam Schwalje 8
Margo Spencer 7
Perry Suszek 2
Brian Tuffnel 1
Donald Vasquez 44

CELLO

George Albeck 25
Betsy Anderson 1
Herb Beenhouwer 1
Michael Brinegar 4
Susan Buchroeder 2
Glenna Carinci 62
Carol Carnicom 16
Rebecca Caron 7
Willard Chilcott 22
Ruth Claire 3
Kathleen Clark 32
Carl Condit 21
Nelson Denman 1
Jody Ellis 86
Elaine Favill 15
Jesse Garcia 1
Chris Ginocchio 4
Sheryl Glasser 12
Paula Gursky 15
Steve Haines 2
Nancy Hauser 15
Deborah Haynes 2
Steve Hess 9
Benjamin Hickman 1
Ztaise Hobbes 1
Marilyn Hoff 1
Judith Ingles 4

David Kaufman 1
Jim Knudson 34
David Kraig 2
Lincoln Leer 12
Laura Locke 1
Gina Matthews 12
Dina Matz 49
Robert Mende 3
Nancy Merson 3
Ray Olson 1
Sueellen Primost 1
Anna Quirk 3
Lisa Rappoport 1
Laurel Rogers 6
Jeff Saltzman 4
Robert Sanders 2
Adam Schwalje 8
Tom Terwilliger 45
Mark Theil 2
Anne Tillery 1
Lisa Walker 16
Erin Whitney 2
Judy Wilson 2
Michael Zachary 2
Sue Ellen Zepeda 5
Helen Zerwas 11

CLARINET

Richard Baldinger 36
Tom Brooks 2
Maria L. Chavez 6
Anne-Lise Cohen 20
David Curtis 10
Caitlin Gannon 1
Dorothy Gjerdrum 4
Alan Glasser 13
Michael Golden 82
Denise Gulliver 1

Chris Hiatt 3
Robert Jones 40
Ralph Lewis 1
Manuel Mandel 6
William Ryburn 7
Richard Snider 18
Bill Spight 12
Sarah Stein 1
Larry Trout 1

CONTRABASSOON

Justin Price 1
Beth Van Arsdel 1

ENGLISH HORN

Dennis Calvin 31
Elaine Heltman 6
Esther Powell 19

FLUTE

Hope Aldrich 2
Winifred Bauer 37
David Bohling 3
Rebecca Carpenter 38
Michael Carroll 2
Ellen Cooke 1
Susan DeJong 1
Marylinda Gutierrez 61
Greta Jones 1
Bruce Lamb 1
Marty Martinez 1
Mary Ann Martinez 90
Ximena Mercado 5
Jane Miller 1
Catie Moore 2
Ler Nelson 3

Emily Nevins 4
Wendy Nunnelley 1
Mamie Jo O'Bryan 47
Linda Rottmann 1
Jeffrey Smedberg 9
Lisa Stuckey 4
Sarma Taylor 2
Karen Watson 13
Patrick Whitesell 1

HORN

John Brockmeyer 20
Melody Brooks 1
Betty Byrd 27
Eli Corin 4
Laura Deanovic 31
William Droke 2
Judy Dudziak 1
Stephanie Fauber 4
Alice Felhau 14
Karol Felts 1
Lisa Fitch 1
Justine Flynn 1
Scott Gerlach 2
Judy Gudziak 1
Sandy Haisley 2
John Hargreaves 1
Roger Henderson 2
Rachel Herr 5
Steve Higgins 7
Elizabeth Hunke 29
Samuel Johnson 3
Carey Johnson 1
Marcie Meyers 8
Steven Ovitsky 7
Howard Pakin 40
Virginia Pannabecker 1
Paul Pease 13

John C. Petring 8
Janet Redman 1
Mark Reis 1
Anthony Sandoval 1
Beth Scott 1
Thomasine Scott 54
Joel Scott 1
Jay Shelton 2
Dori Smith 1
Nathan Stark 4
Robert Stevens 6
Nissa Strottman 3
Thaddeus Sze 5
Mateel Todd 1
Johann Trujillo 7
J. Turley 1
Alysia Williams 6
Shelley Winship 1
Lara Wirtz 5
Mariel Yelm 1

HARP

Gail Bass 1
Anne Eisfeller 1
Lynn Gorman 3
Bill Grabowski 12
Gail Ross 1
Sheila Schiferl 7
Melodie Schneider 3
Rosalind Simpson 4

OBOE

Irene Alexander 3
Patrick Berry 25
Dennis Calvin 31
Katherine Campbell 12
Elizabeth Doyle-Bunch 1

David Dunn 3
Kim Euston 4
Freddie Feterspiel 1
Barrett Flaschar 2
Gerry Fried 32
April Gerlach 5
Elaine Heltman 6
Dan Koenig 36
Kathleen Lash 11
Robert Pena 1
Susan Petring 1
Esther Powell 19
Ashley Reid 5
Charles Rzeszutko 9
Jon Schneider 25
Dana Simmons 1
Elizabeth White 1
Rebeka Yozell-Epstein 1

PERCUSSION

Sharon Adams 2
Sarah Angel 4
John Bartlett 1
Amy Beegle 1
Loren Bienvenu 1
Kip Bischofberger 2
Chandra Blackston 2
Stuart Bloom 20
Stephen Bloom 4
Robert Borton 2
Roger Brooks 3
Marty Buchsbaum 9
Michael Carroll 2
James Compton 3
Suzanne Cooter 4
Laura Deanovic 31
Julia Drahn 9
Terry Edwards 1

George Fellows 1
Johnny Finn 2
Cole Fredricks 2
Gerald Garcia 1
Eric Gent 2
Anita Gerlach 10
April Gerlach 5
Elena Gomez 6
Heidi Greiser 1
Cal Haines 3
Mary-Kay Henderson 1
Ann Hey 1
Tom Holien 2
David Hollander 1
Doug Hoover 1
Gene Hutchinson 1
Ranjit Khalsa 1
Nick Kunz 1
Sam Lunt 2
Desi Martinez 2
Wendy McGuire 50
Jennifer McLaughlin 5
Cain Miller 2
Richard Money 1
Carl Necker 1
Andrew Primm 1
Maureen Reyer 1
Woody Rubin 6
Brian Stengel 1
Len Stovall 8
Cindy Turner 3
David Wildes 3

PIANO

Peggy Abbott 1
Richard Christensen 3
Ron Grinage 1
Lydia Madrick 1

Kelvin McNeal 2
Mila Murray 1
Richard Reichman 1
John Roberts 1
Patrice Foster Williams 3

TROMBONE

David Aleguire 1
Edie Baldinger 7
Mariah Bennett 7
Stanley Birge 1
Bill Britton 3
Larry Bronisz 1
James Brown 4
Elizabeth Burk 1
Douglas Camp 1
Dennis Clason 6
Scott Crane 1
Cole Fredricks 2
Jan Gaynor 1
Bruce Herr 10
Bruce Hiatt 1
D.J. Jennison 1
Phil Jones 13
Bob Kasenchak 3
G. S. Khalsa 8
Dorothy Kincaid 47
Ricky Korzekwa 2
John Luther 2
Walter McClendon 2
Jerry Morzinski 7
Calvin Moss 15
Kyle Nekimken 1
Richard Noll 5
Michael Pollock 1
Nick Pulaski 7
David Roe 1
Rick Sena 3

Jason Settlemoir 1
Allen Stein 1
David Stephan 1
Jason Sulliman 2
Steven Trujillo 1
Ted Vives 23
Bill Wilkes 2
Al Williams 3
Eva Woody 7
Beth Yip 1

TRUMPET

Pat Heinz Anderson 1
Casey Anderson 1
Wayne Buschmann 6
Dean Decker 4
Paul Deininger 4
Jim Dell 5
Michael Ebinger 43
Xavier Fernandez 8
Linda Foster 1
Kathy Fulton 1
Kent Garret 4
Veronica Garza 2
Nathan George 1
Kurt Hackbarth 1
Robin Harney 2
Pat Heinz 4
Greg Heltman 17
Brian Hertz 3
Larry Hill 1
Steve Hollahan 1
Joe Holland 1
John Hollander 1
Jan-Willem Jansens 4
Robert Krakowski 5
Matthew Krum 1
Nate Kruse 2

Bruce Letellier 3
Jan McDonald 1
Bill McGehee 3
Mario Montoya 11
Pete Murray 12
Miguel Navarot 1
Vic Perry 38
Claudia Pozel 1
Garth Ramsey 1
Kareen Reyer 1
Cheryl Rodriguez 3
Alfred Romero 1
Rose Sanchez 3
Russell Scharf 6
Jim Toevs 2
Michael Wagner 10
Scott Wagner 1
Bob Woody 1

TUBA

Richard Anaya 4
David Marble 9
Jim Martinez 4
Jerry Morzinski 7
David O'Kane 1
Neal Palmer 1
Steve Ross 19
Gary Sherman 1

VIOLA

Carolyn Albers 1
Doug Alde 5
Archer Ames 5
Ann Anastasio 1
Deborah Bluestone 2
Delronda Boyd 3
David Brown 13

James Bunch 55
Kathleen Clark 32
John DiJanni 4
Pat Gamble 3
Giselle Garcia 1
Pat Greathouse 41
Kathy Gursky 4
Maggie Hagen 2
Steve Hess 9
Art Hopkins 11
Preston Hutchins 5
Marla Karmesin 21
Carl Laukkanen 2
Lincoln Leer 12
Jean Luther 4
Melissa Lyans 3
Ann Martin 4
Catherine Matovich 2
Kok Heong McNaughton 57
Julie Meadows 1
Jack Miller 5
David Mulberry 25
Kathleen Neher 1
E. J. Nelson 8
Nan Newton 3
Betsy Odgers 1
Linnea Ohlsen 25
Nicole Osterhaus 3
Christine Pacheco 1
Tina Park 1
Elizabeth Poe 9
Audrey Powers 7
Oliver Prezant 2
Britt Ravnan 28
Ellen Ravnan 1
Kater Reynolds 1
James Rives 4
Marilyn Rohn 2
John Runner 3

Karles Saucedo-McQuade 1
Kathleen Schallock 30
Salome Solano 8
Marke Talley 15
Jean Thomas 14
Robin Thompson 1
Claire Vanderberg 1
Steina Vasulka 32
Marianne Walck 2
Marcia Walrath 5
John Ward 29
Jesse Watson 1
Tom Weber 7
Deborah Weltzer 1

VIOLIN

Bob Albers 1
Isaac Allen 6
Andrew Anda 2
Linda Armer 26
Margaret Armstrong 39
Corey Bachman 1
Bill Bailey 1
Cathy Barba 2
Dale Barber 17
Susan Bodishbaugh 1
Rita Brooks 4
James Bunch 55
Suzie Burton 2
Andrew Cameron 5
Leslie Campos 1
Lynn Case 9
Mary-Ray Cate 2
David Charles 2
Melissa Cimino 9
Torsten Clay 1
Elizabeth Cohen 3
Janet Cordova 40

Elaine Davidson 3
Audrey Davis 22
Cissy Quay de la Vallee 37
Larry DeToth 2
Hillary DiCecco 2
Anita Dunham 1
Jonathan Dunn 8
Anne Hays Egan 14
Richard Elias 1
Stephen Elliott 1
Jennifer Elliott 45
Ivi Esquerra 1
Christine Evertsz 3
Mary Ann Fellows 2
Keri Felts 12
Francine Fields 2
Therese Francis 6
Toby Gass 28
Harold Geller 78
Bobbie Gibson 1
Andrea Glasgow 1
Pat Greathouse 41
Michael Greene 1
Janet Hamm 3
Diane Harris 6
Lee Harvey 32
Mildred Hemsing 1
Sky Hitt 1
Ian Holmes 2
Bob Honea 1
Ed Hyde 16
Gabriele James 4
Tom Juster 58
Gail Kaplan 51
Marla Karmesin 21
Sharron Kenty 8
Martha Dean Kerr 69
Annie Kuzava 20
Josette Laforge 1

Marilyn LaForge 6
Beth Lambert 1
Tom Leith 17
Clea Lopez 1
Beryl Lovitz 9
Melissa Lucas-Huckabee 1
William Madlan 1
Michelle Madland 1
Paul Malmuth 2
Catherine Matovich 2
Richlyn McArthur 8
Kok Heong McNaughton 57
Lisa Merrill 1
Roger Miller 4
Robin Miziumski 1
Kathleen Mower 5
Maureen Mullaney 1
Alice Mutschlechner 4
Peggy Nelson 4
Brian Newnam 3
Linnea Ohlsen 25
Cathy Owen 1
Marian Pack 2
Marilyn Page 5
Richard Palazzolo 3
Marc Pearson 1
Janet Pederson 1
Michael Polera 2
Justin Pollak 12
Britt Ravnan 28
Judith Reno 3
Debbie Risberg 1
Gail Robertson 9
Susan Robinson 2
Kristie Ross 26
Dolly Sax 10
Sitara Schauer 1
Lucille Schmuhl 1
Pat Schriber 7

Don Schwimmer 7
Audrey Setterland 2
Cheryl Smith-Ecke 1
Sandy Snider 8
Alan Soper 1
Elena Sopoci 1
Janet Steinberg 20
Shirley Steiner 5
Rob Stenseth 28
Rebecca Stradling 1
Robert Suhre 1
Rahimah Sultan 5
Pam Tech 5
Gillian Telfer 5
Marsha Thomas 1
Jean Thomas 14
Pat Tillery 1
Cathy Todd 2
Larry Toth 8
Jim Ummel 1
Bernie van der Hoeven 16
Jean Van Duong 1
Lisa Van Sickle 74
Steina Vasulka 32
Janet Veach 1
Lucia Vorys 4
Eleanore Voutselas 9
Marianne Walck 2
Robert Walpole 30
Charmaine Weber 2
Tom Weber 7
Jane Ann Welch 14
Kathryn Wendt 26
Sue White 4
Linda Whitney 1
Maria Widen 1
Susan Wider 4
Gloria Wilson 3
Jada Yuan 1